The
Little Gardener

The
Little Gardener

HELPING CHILDREN CONNECT WITH THE NATURAL WORLD

Julie A. Cerny

ILLUSTRATIONS BY YSEMAY DERCON

PRINCETON ARCHITECTURAL PRESS
NEW YORK

for Mom and Dad

and the trees

GROWING YOUR GARDEN

TEACHING & LEARNING IN YOUR GARDEN

"See deeply the beauty and
interconnectedness of all life;
then think, speak and act
from what you see."

Maggie Streincrohn Davis
Caring in Remembered Ways

INTRODUCTION

When I was a young girl, I often dreamed of sitting in the center of a circular garden. I wanted to feel like just a speck among towering flower stalks—small and still, totally surrounded by growing things. While the flowers and I basked in the sun's warmth and light, I radiated with delight and satisfaction knowing I had planted them all myself.

I have always loved being outside. Gardens and wild nature have been a part of my life for as long as I can remember. Until I was ten, a quarter of our tiny backyard was home to tomatoes, cucumbers, mint, and more. On summer days, I would play in the shade of the lean-to-style cucumber trellis and then happily take charge of the garden hose—"rescuing" tomato plants from the heat of the day. Growing up, my family would camp out at a small hunting cabin. On the land there, my sister Susan and

I would spend countless hours exploring the woods, building forts, and playing in streams.

Since then, I've savored living and working in places where I can *feel* the elements seeping into my life, places where I'm reminded daily that the natural world is at once incredibly beautiful and fiercely indomitable, and where I am challenged to explore where nature ends and I begin.

I began working as an outdoor educator fifteen years ago. In cities, at summer camps, in town parks, in state forests, and in the wilderness, I guided youth through experiences studying ponds, hiking mountains, and playing games that illustrated how natural systems work. Together we would walk silently in the dark, snowshoe across frozen ponds, identify trees by bark and bud, inspect animal tracks in mud and snow, map ecosystems, and splash stream water on our faces. I saw hundreds of children light up inside.

Children were intrigued as they observed pond water under a microscope. Hiking mountains was awe inspiring. Playing games was an exciting way to learn key ecological concepts. Nature became a friendlier and more familiar place.

Though I saw these children lighting up inside, and knew the experiences were meaningful to them, as an educator I was concerned that these activities weren't doing enough to connect them to nature in a deep and personal way—or cultivate an understanding of where human beings fit into ecological systems. I realized that nature was still a "place" to them. Nature was still an "other."

It wasn't until I saw children in a garden—holding seeds, planting them, touching the soil, and smelling, harvesting, and tasting food (nature)—that I knew they were truly perceiving their place in the natural world. And it made perfect sense. The most direct and intimate way to connect with nature is, clearly, to eat it. A small part of it becomes a small part of you—and it fills you up a little more every time. Eventually you begin to realize that you have always been 100 percent nature, that you are made of the same components of all that you see in the natural world—your body made of water and carbon, same as the flower stalks. Gardens remind us that everything is connected, and that "everything" includes us.

Many schools are still missing the mark when it comes to teaching students that everything is as intricately, deeply, and beautifully connected as it is. Young people generally learn math separate from science, science separate from history, history separate from writing, writing separate from health, and health separate from the next thing. And, we have actual walls between where we teach each of these subjects. WALLS!

As an outdoor teacher, I've had wonderful opportunities to walk with students across these boundaries, and maybe even knock bricks off a few walls. Gardens have provided more of these opportunities for me and my students than any other setting I've worked in. Seeing so many Little Gardeners lose themselves among towering flower stalks, or grow, harvest, and taste fresh food—crisp sugar snap peas, cherry tomatoes that burst in their mouths, or the curiously tart cucamelon—I am drawn to the sparks that fly, reigniting connections to nature that have faded, been long lost, or never had the opportunity to form at all.

Gardening cultivates ecological literacy—a working knowledge of how ecological systems support all life on this planet. When we garden, it's easier to see ourselves as part of those systems and to experience firsthand how our choices affect our environment, for better or for worse. Young gardeners are more likely to have increased positive environmental attitudes and are more apt to notice (and care) that some of the choices humans make are creating severe environmental problems.

Through gardening, young people discover that their own hands can affect their well-being, the well-being of others, and, accomplished with intention and care, the well-being of natural systems. They come to know their own ability to engage with ecosystems, steward life, and change the world. And they will be better equipped to handle the salient environmental issues we face.

Gardens are clearly not the only place where this kind of experiential eco-literacy education can take place, but, it's where I've witnessed the most inspiring interactions between people and nature. And it gives me hope that human beings can work with nature to create joy and abundance for our own existence and not undermine nature's own wellness while doing so.

The Little Gardener is part how to create and grow a garden, part guide to using your garden as a teaching tool, and part inspiration for promoting ecological literacy and cultivating nature's keepers through gardening. You will be guided through envisioning your dream garden, setting intentions and goals for the garden you will create, designing the garden and bringing it to life, and harvesting and eating what you and nature have grown together.

This is not a book about fast and easy gardening, although such tips will be offered. I make the assumption that you and your Little Gardener are up for crafting your garden in a very intentional way and are willing to invest time and energy in making it a meaningful part of your lives. Given the detail offered (brevity has never been my strong suit), this book will enable you to do just that.

As you and your Little Gardener embark on your gardening journey, remember that there are no two places on Earth with the exact same conditions of soil, climate, weather, topography, culture, and history. Answers to gardening questions are rarely completely right or wholly wrong; "it depends" is generally the smartest answer. The best way to learn about gardening where you live is to talk to other gardeners in your area—the oldest ones you can find.

Before you begin, know that a garden can live in a bucket. It can live in a backyard, a front yard, or the small strips of earth between roads and sidewalks. It can live on a windowsill. While this book focuses on gardens that are bigger than a bucket or a windowsill, the main concepts presented can easily be adapted to cozier spaces. Grow wherever you can. It will be worthwhile.

HOW TO USE THIS BOOK

The Little Gardener will take you and your Little Gardener on a step-by-step journey of creating a garden and connecting with nature. While intended to be read and experienced in chronological order, once you start to get a feel for what *The Little Gardener* is all about, I suggest looking ahead at "Teaching & Learning in the Garden." It will help you feel out how to "become" Big Gardener—Little Gardener's guide in the garden.

This Book Is for Both of You

If you have the time and it works well for you, read a chapter through first, then share it with Little Gardener and work through the activities together. (All activities can be adjusted to work well for Little Gardeners of almost any age.) You'll find that certain parts of the main text are simple enough for Little Gardener to understand. Don't miss the "Just for Little Gardener" sidebars—you may choose to read these aloud or let Little Gardener enjoy exploring them solo.

Help Along the Journey

Extra gardening advice, explorations of ecological systems, and reading recommendations (for each of you) are peppered throughout the book, and additional educational and gardening resources are provided in the back.

Garden Journals

To guide you along the way, I offer journal prompts and reminders to record your observations, make important notes, and reflect on your gardening journey. I encourage you to use your journaling time mindfully—it's a wonderful opportunity to note and recognize how your relationship with nature may be shifting as you spend more and more time with your plants, with the soil, and with nature. This journal can become your steadfast companion as you and Little Gardener grow alongside your garden.

AUTHOR'S NOTE

On most days, I think and feel that humans and gardens are both natural. Humans are members of the animal kingdom and gardening is a way we cocreate with nature. Despite this, when I use the terms "natural systems" and "ecological systems" in this book (interchangeably) to define systems that are nonhuman, or exclaim that through gardening we can restore human connections to the ecological systems that sustain us, I imply that we are separate from them. It would be more accurate to say that I believe we are and have always been part of natural systems—but we have a lot of work to do in reminding ourselves of this. It is my hope that *The Little Gardener* will serve as a reminder that we *are* nature.

On the other days, I am challenged by a few glaring facts which indicate humans and gardens are unnatural. In nature, there is no waste, something humans excel at creating. Plants and wild creatures take what they need to survive—we take much, much more. While gardens, cultivated nature, may need us to survive, I don't believe wild nature does.

Regardless of how you define nature or if you agree with the above perspectives, you will find *The Little Gardener* helpful in crafting a beautiful, nourishing garden and cultivating conscious connections to the natural world.

DREAMING YOUR GARDEN

VISUALIZING

Unearth your creativity

The most memorable gardens I know—the most beautiful and inspiring ones—are the gardens that invite me in. They blur the lines between what feels cultivated and what feels wild. They hold space for humans as well as habitat for a variety of creatures, and are integrated into the natural systems around them.

When we go searching for our place in the natural world, spaces like these are often where we find ourselves. They are living reminders that animals (including humans) and plants, gardens and the wild, all rely on natural systems. Nature invites us in because we, like all other creatures, are intrinsically connected to it. We *are* it.

In gardens, where the gardener's well-being is intertwined with that of the garden, we are reminded of this connection. In these spaces, only vague boundaries exist between where the plants grow and where the caretaker lives, and humans are more steward-inhabitants than invited guests. Gardens like these do some of the best work of encouraging Little Gardeners to be nature's keepers.

On the far side of an open farm field, the garden was sound asleep beneath a pure, white, undulating crust of snow. It was January in New York's Upper Hudson Valley, and we were in the thick of an unusually snowy winter. It would be a good while before I could get a look at the earth beneath. This was my introduction to The Sylvia Center's Learning Garden, a garden that I would have the opportunity to design, care for, and teach in, and I was eager to get started. There was so much I wanted to know about the garden:

What was the composition and texture of the soil?

How did water, wind, and sunlight move across the land?

Exactly how much cultivated space was there?

How wide were the beds and paths?

Were there any perennials? Where had they been planted?

What made this piece of land great for gardening?

What about this land was challenging?

Planning out the growing season for a sight-unseen garden is no easy task. Information about the layout was limited, as were records of what had been grown in prior seasons. Because it was unfenced, I could only guess at its edges and general shape. What I did know was that for three years the space had been managed as an educational garden that grew enough produce such that groups as large as sixty students could harvest ingredients to prepare their own lunches throughout the growing season.

Until the snow began to melt and the garden woke up, I wouldn't have much data to work with. Instead, I used the extra time to align myself more deeply with the garden's purpose—visualizing the space and setting intentions that would guide the processes of designing and planning.

The Sylvia Center, a nonprofit educational organization based in New York City, was founded in 2007 with the purpose of providing opportunities for children of all demographics, abilities, and walks of life to experience the joy, health, and wellness that comes from growing, preparing, and enjoying fresh food. Each year, the center's culinary and food literacy programs serve several thousand young people and their families in schools, community spaces, public housing, and on Katchkie Farm in the Learning Garden and outdoor kitchen.

The Sylvia Center's primary mission is to "inspire children to eat well" and "grow communities of healthy eaters" through hands-on experiences of growing and preparing fresh food. The distinct mission of the Learning Garden, within the center's broader mission, is to provide young people with meaningful and unforgettable experiences with fresh, healthy food by fostering connections to where it comes from and how it grows.

Students visiting the garden would participate in every step of the story of food: preparing the soil, planting seeds, tending to seedlings, transplanting them, cultivating garden beds, spreading compost, pruning plants, harvesting fresh ingredients, preparing food, and eating it. As big gardeners and little gardeners, big naturalists and little naturalists, big chefs and little chefs, big eaters and little eaters, we would create, work, and learn together. It was a dream job. And it was time to dream up a garden that would make all of this possible.

I envisioned a garden that would inspire and encourage children to reconsider who they were, where they were, and what was happening around them. I wanted to create a place where they would feel awed by a reality in which the walls between humans and nature were not quite so high and the forgotten connections between the two were effortless to perceive, a place where children could tune in to how their bodies responded to being outside, harvesting nature, and eating it. By engaging with seeds, soil, and living food, they could come to recognize their ability to create health and well-being for themselves. They would have an opportunity to directly experience how the natural world nurtures us and understand why it's important that we nurture it in return.

Over the course of six years, the garden would become this exact place. It would become the setting for me and several thousand Big and Little Gardeners, as well as teachers and learners, to embark on a heart-stirring adventure of cocreation.

WHAT DO YOU WANT <u>YOUR</u> GARDEN TO BE?

Before we continue the story of how the Learning Garden came to be, and before we get caught up in the forthcoming nitty-gritty details of how your family might go about designing a garden that connects you with the natural world, let's first focus on understanding your purpose, creating a mission statement, and then visualizing your family's dream garden.

Your garden can be big or small, simple or extravagant, a garden that fills your backyard or just a few herbs

SETTING INTENTIONS

Anytime you plan to create something, it's helpful to imagine what it will look like before you start. It's also important to understand your reason for wanting to create that thing. Having a clear idea of what you would like to create and why you would like to do so, will help you stay focused on creating what you have dreamed. Grown-ups sometimes call this "setting intentions."

growing on your sunny windowsill. Whatever space you have, it will be just right.

Your garden mission statement expresses in broad, general terms what you are trying to accomplish by having a garden.

Maybe you think gardens are beautiful, or you'd like to have fresh tomatoes and basil a few steps from your kitchen. Perhaps it's important to you to become more self-sufficient or live more sustainably. Maybe you're concerned about the scarcity of habitat and food sources for butterflies or bees, our endangered pollinators. Maybe being in a garden simply brings you peace. Maybe you're a teacher or are homeschooling your children and want your garden to serve as an outdoor teaching space.

A garden well-loved by an entire family or community will inevitably be and do so much. Nothing in nature operates independently of anything else. Everything is connected. Everything has more than one function. And so, too, will your garden. That said, it's important to have at least an informal mission statement that you can return to as you embark on your own adventure of cocreation.

ACTIVITIES

WRITING A GARDEN MISSION STATEMENT

Having a garden journal can be invaluable in all stages of your gardening adventure. Grab two blank notebooks, one for Big Gardener and one for Little Gardener. Pencils, too. (Having crayons or colored pencils close by is not a bad idea either.)

Take a moment to reflect on the following questions and record your thoughts. This will help you to create your statement.

· Why does your family want to create a garden?
· What are your passions and values as they relate to having a garden?

An example of a mission statement for your garden might be, "Our garden grows fresh food for our family and is a place where we can sit peacefully in nature," or "Our garden is a place where we can explore our connections to nature by cultivating fruits, vegetables, and flowers." Take time to discover what feels right and true for you and your family.

Write your mission statement down in a prominent place in your garden journal. When it comes time to make another decision about your garden, revisit this mission statement to see which choice most closely aligns with your original intention. If you begin to feel like your garden is naturally drifting away from your mission statement, it's more than fine to adjust the statement rather than your garden. Your garden will always be evolving and growing, just like you and your family.

VISUALIZING A GARDEN
THAT INVITES YOU IN

It's time to put aside practical matters, forget about what you think is or isn't possible, and remember that it's called *dreaming* for a reason.

Take turns reading the following out loud to each other, while the listener visualizes her dream garden. (If Little Gardener is too young to read to Big Gardener, consider asking a friend or family member to help. If Little Gardener is very little, consider choosing just a few of the questions to focus on.)

Close your eyes. Take a few deep, mindful breaths.

Imagine walking into your garden. Move slowly.

Notice the sounds around you. What do you hear?

What's the temperature like? Do you feel sunshine on your skin?

Notice the path that you are walking on. Is it bare earth, wood chips, pebbles, grass, stone? How does it feel under your feet?

What else do you see nearby? Is there a tree you'd like to sit under or a bench to rest on? What colors do you see?

What foods are growing in the garden beds? What is ready to eat right now? Pick one. What does it feel like in your hand? Eat it. What does it taste like? Are there berry bushes, fruit trees, nut trees?

Where do you want to play and explore?

What kinds of insects, birds, and other creatures live in your garden?

Is there space in your garden to camp out under the stars?

Are there flowers blooming? What kinds or what colors? Go smell a few of them. What do they smell like?

Take a few more deep breaths.

How do you feel? What about your garden is making you feel this way?

In your garden journal, write, draw, or collage about your experience of walking through your dream garden. Share your stories and/or pictures with each other, as well as with friends and family.

SPARKING MORE GARDEN IMAGINING

Here are some other ways you and your Little Gardener can dream more deeply about your garden to be:

- Visit your local library and look through gardening books together (especially ones with lots of pictures).

- Visit a community garden.

- Request seed catalogs be mailed to you. (See page 218 for a list of seed companies.)

- Imagine what your garden will look like in winter, spring, summer, and fall. Then draw or write a story about your garden in each season.

JOURNAL PROMPTS

- What first sparked your interest in having a garden?
- What aspect of gardening are you most excited about?
- Why is it important to have a mission statement and consult it regularly?
- What is the deeper reason you want to succeed at your garden's mission?

CHAPTER REVIEW

- Gardening gives us a direct experience of the natural world nurturing us, and shows us why it's important that we nurture it in return.

- Before you create a garden, put reality aside for a moment and simply visualize how you would like your garden to look and feel.

- Your garden mission statement will help you stay closely connected to your dream garden.

IN THE NEXT CHAPTER...

Smile. You've dreamt up a garden that invites you in. The next step is perhaps the most important one in creating a garden, but it is often overlooked: you must get to know the environment that your garden will be a part of. Connecting with your land through deep observation and spending time mindfully gathering data will help you to forge a deeper relationship with the outdoors, to consider how certain environmental factors may affect your garden, and to choose a site where your garden is most likely to thrive.

CHAPTER TWO
DISCOVERING

Connect with the land

My parents are baby boomers, and, as kids, when they weren't at school they were outside. All day. They were riding bikes, building forts, making mud pies, helping with yard and garden work, fishing, exploring, hanging out in treehouses, swimming, playing games, and running around with friends. Weather was nearly irrelevant.

They'd go inside to eat, sleep, read, listen to the radio, do chores, or do their homework. But the really exciting stuff was happening outside. And because engaging with the outdoors was part of their lifestyle, they were more observant of and more deeply connected to the natural systems that live there. When we are out in nature, and are quiet enough for long enough, we can keenly sense the unspoken understanding between our bodies and soil, our bodies and water, our bodies and the sun.

Gardening lets us tap into something within us that recognizes these relationships as vital to our survival—and we are hardwired to survive. Deep down, we know that everything is connected. What we do in the garden and what we do more broadly to our environment affects how much nourishment and fulfillment we and other living things can receive from it.

As we spend less time outdoors and feel less of a connection to where our food and other resources come from, we seem to lose touch with this instinctive understanding. And I believe the best way to reconnect is through gardening.

OUR ROLE IN THE GREAT DISCONNECT

Amidst the busyness of our lives, it's easy to lose track of how much time we and our children are spending inside, not to mention in front of screens. We increasingly try to satisfy our innate desire to play, experiment, and explore with two-dimensional stimuli. Instead of observing and gathering information about our physical surroundings, we are gathering "likes" on social media and berries to feed Pokémon. The gratification we receive from screens, in concert with the relatively new ability to access information instantly, disconnects us from raw, real-world experiences that fuel our curiosity to learn.

Technology isn't the only thing stealing the show either. As our young ones splash through puddles, we often request they don't. As they wander past where our eyes can see, we often beckon them back to us. We do this because it simply makes sense, for safety, or sometimes just because it makes our lives easier, which is certainly understandable—the inconvenience of going through several changes of clothes may try one's patience. That said, as adults, we must acknowledge our contribution to the disconnect between our children and nature.

I encourage you to try letting go, *ever* so slightly, and in whatever way feels most doable for you—because I believe you, too, may remember that the best explorations of nature often happen beyond where parents are watching.

THE JOY & IMPORTANCE OF RECONNECTING

For some of us, nature in its wildest forms can be found right at our doorstep, the vast workings of natural systems in plain sight. Those who live farther from the wilds of nature can, if they look, find examples of ecological systems at work too. Often, though, our daily or weekly routines do not consciously and deeply connect us with nature. It's not easy for us to see where our life-giving resources come from.

Spending time interacting with nature helps us forge a relationship with ecological systems and how they support us. How often during your day do your surroundings remind you that everything you do depends on the health of soil, air, and water? How different might our world be if taking an introductory course in ecological literacy was a requirement for high school graduation? What opportunities are offered to young people to observe the natural world and develop an understanding of what sustains all life on this planet?

If we don't understand where natural resources come from, how can we ensure they will always be there for us? With deliberate intention and observation, we can stay connected to the natural principles in action that are supporting us and all other life, no matter where we live. Live closer to and rely more directly on these systems, and you will feel a new part of yourself come alive.

CULTIVATING LITTLE GARDENER'S CONNECTION TO NATURE

Imagine yourself watching Little Gardener harvest and eat fresh berries first thing in the morning. Imagine seeing the lettuce you've planted together perk up on a rainy afternoon following a dry spell. Imagine discovering a bird's nest among cucumber vines. These moments stir something vital in us. While not more or less significant than having a picnic in the park, going for a day hike, or spending an afternoon bird-watching, cocreating a garden with nature offers us far more opportunities, through direct observation and engagement, to develop conscious connections to nature. Gardening teaches us how to support, cultivate, and even regenerate natural systems.

In my experience working as an outdoor educator with thousands of kids over a period of fifteen years, it's become clear to me that children who grow up on farms or with vegetable gardens tend to "get it." When they work with plants, animals, weather, and soil on a daily basis, they grow up as members of the ecological systems that sustain them. They develop a more comprehensive, nuanced, and meaningful relationship with the natural world—and they do so without a single formal lesson.

Working the land was once a defining characteristic of American culture and society. Over the last century, however, a rural farm lifestyle—growing your own food, harvesting firewood for fuel, being directly responsible for building and maintaining your own shelter, and creating marketable products from your land base—has become a dying livelihood. Despite the "back to the land" movements, the percentage of the American population who lives on farms has declined significantly over the last one hundred years. And while the number of young farmers is on the rise, there are currently not enough of them to replace the oldest generation and reverse the downward trend.

Both in my personal life and through working with young people, I have found that the wonder of discovering what can come from working with our own hands and with nature is distinctly moving to our spirits. For the young people who at first might not understand their own connection to nature, the "ah-ha!" moments happen when they eat food that they participated in growing. There is something profoundly joyful and deeply fulfilling about being responsible for where our own sustenance comes from, and then sharing that sustenance with others.

NO TWO PLACES ARE THE SAME

In starting your own garden, you'll have to learn to work with the unique environment your land has to offer. This is the essence of gardening. Our world is a grand assortment of countless diverse systems engaging with each other. Climate, weather, soils, water, biology, plant physiology, and chemistry are just a few of the components that make up the world we live in. Depending on where you live, these systems vary widely. And they may vary widely even within your space.

I've grown food and taught Little Gardeners on educational farms and gardens in two very different climates: on a dry mesa at 9,000 feet in Colorado's San Juan Mountains, and on two

EMBRACE YOUR GARDENING SPACE #1

The Sylvia Center Learning Garden lives out in the fields of Katchkie Farm, a commercial organic vegetable farm a handful of miles east of the Hudson River in Kinderhook, New York. Prior to the completion of a massive drainage project, the land was unworkably wet. And without the addition of copious amounts of organic matter, the soil would have remained a relatively hard clay with no hope of successfully growing much of anything. On the other hand, with a slight slope to the west and full southern exposure, the Learning Garden tends to warm up nicely with the return of the sun each spring and has the longest frost-free season of anywhere I've grown vegetables.

different farms in New York State, one in the Hudson River Valley and one in the upper Taconic Valley. Each farm was distinctly gorgeous. Each farm welcomed visitors of all ages and abilities. And each farm's land had unique strengths and challenges when it came to growing vegetables. Throughout this chapter, you'll find summaries of what it was like to cocreate with these different pieces of land. I hope these short narratives will inspire you to understand and appreciate your space in new ways.

GETTING TO KNOW THE SYLVIA CENTER LEARNING GARDEN

That first season at the Learning Garden, after the snow had melted and before the ground had fully thawed, I was out and about with my measuring tape, figuring out exactly how much growing space I had to work with. As winter closed and spring progressed, I watched carefully for which areas thawed

JUST FOR LITTLE GARDENER
FINDING THE RIGHT SPOT

Choosing a spot for your garden is
an important decision. Look for areas
that get lots of sun and where the
soil is not too wet. Can you imagine
taking the time to build a whole
garden only to find out it was not
the best place for vegetables to grow
after all?

first and which stayed frozen the longest. When spring rains came, I watched for where puddles lingered and noted which areas dried out first. I observed and sensed which spaces felt protected or exposed.

While my garden already had borders, a shape, and some perennials growing, you may have the opportunity to start a brand-new garden. And if you have that wonderful opportunity, there are some important things to think about when choosing where to put it. Being a close observer of your space is one of the most effective ways to learn to read your environment and to find the best spot for your garden.

OBSERVING & CONNECTING WITH YOUR SPACE

You probably already know a bit about your space—whether it's a postage-stamp backyard or a big open lawn—like where to find the coolest shade on a hot summer afternoon, the best spot for playing games, or maybe your dog's favorite place to dig in the dirt!

It's time to get to know your environment on an even deeper level. The following topics and assessment questions will help you develop your "gardener's eyes" to make observations that will guide you in choosing the best site for your garden. Invest in this step. The more legwork you do at this stage of the game, the easier it will be to create a garden that thrives.

Sunlight
Watch how the sunshine and shadows travel across your space throughout the year. Is there a space that gets a minimum of six hours of direct sunlight for the entirety of your growing season (between your last and first frosts)? More sunlight than that?

Even better! Garden vegetables need plenty of light to live and produce. With good planning and a little creativity, you can increase shade in your garden, but more sunshine is a tall order. Be mindful of any trees that may grow larger and eventually create more shade.

Water

There is a certain romanticism that accompanies the carrying of watering cans. This feeling will wear off quickly, depending on how far your garden is from your water source, the size of your garden, and how dry of a season awaits you. For plants on a windowsill or pots on a porch, a watering can will be perfectly sufficient. For gardens further from your dwelling, it is of utmost importance that you have a hose that can reach your garden. Having a spigot right in the garden is certainly the most ideal solution but can be costly. How many gallons of water will flow per minute from your water source? If you have a shallow well or are subject to water restrictions, be mindful of how large a garden is sensible.

Soil

Healthy gardens grow in healthy soil. Get up close and personal with your soil by digging a few holes in different areas.

HELPFUL HINT
SAFE DIGGING!

While most garden projects won't require you to dig very deeply into your soil, should you decide to dig any major holes as part of soil exploration or garden creation, be sure to identify the location of your septic tank (if you have one), and any underground pipes and/or wires first! No matter where in the United States you live, you can call 8-1-1 to find out if there are any underground utility lines you should be aware of.

HELPFUL HINT

GET TO KNOW YOUR SOIL

Soil tests can be helpful in getting to know the makeup of your soil, although I've met some gardeners who have never used them and don't care to. If you prefer to keep things simple, purchase a soil pH test kit at your local garden center.

If you want to know all of the juicy details about your soil, check with your county's cooperative extension (an agriculture information and education service) about professional soil-testing services. These inexpensive tests check for the acidity (pH) of the soil, the amount of nutrients and minerals available for plant growth, and the percent of organic matter. Unless you suspect issues with your soil, it's generally best to get your soil tested after establishing your garden plot because you want your sample to be of the soil composition that your plants will be growing in (not a sample filled with grass or other plant matter that may be removed before planting).

Have Little Gardener get down into the soil with you—get your hands into it. What does it feel like? What does it look like? Are there worms, insects, grubs? Does it look alive? How far can you dig before hitting rock or very rough soil? What else are you observing? Record your findings in your journal.

You can also discover more about the health and composition of your soil by identifying and learning about the plants that grow there already. The needs of naturally occurring plants will provide clues about what your soil already has to offer. (You'll learn more about soil in chapter six.)

Site history

If possible, do a little detective work and find out what was happening on your land before your time there. Were there any commercial, industrial, or other activities that may have affected the soil or water?

If you are creating your garden in an urban area, on a site that has been used for industrial or commercial purposes, or is very close to a road, there are special soil issues that you should be aware of—and a standard soil test won't be sufficient. You'll want to have your soil tested for common contaminants, including lead and arsenic, *before* you move forward with your garden plans.

The Environmental Protection Agency has an educational factsheet called "Reusing Potentially Contaminated Landscapes: Growing Gardens in Urban Soils," which can help you identify and mitigate risks associated with gardening in urban areas (see page 218).

Wind

When I'm gardening on windy days, I'm reminded of Dean Leith Jr. who paraphrased Dick Raymond from the *Joy of Gardening* when he commented, "Plants are like people. They catch a cold.

Wyomanock Farm and Wyomanock Center for Sustainable Living (collectively known as WYO) in Stephentown, New York, sits along the Wyomanock Creek, just west of the Berkshires of Massachusetts. The soil there is rich with organic matter and free of rocks, and working it was a dream. But the farm is in a low spot, and cold air always finds its way to the low spots. Winter comes earlier, and snow and ice linger longer there, in part due to the low elevation, and in part due to the neighbor's high tree line of white pines to the south.

On farms, homesteads, or land with extensive gardens, few things are more precious than a reliable water source. At WYO, a crystal-clear spring reliably runs year-round.

They windburn and sunburn. I often lick some tricky garden problems just by putting myself in *their* place."

Exposure to consistent wind can be hard on your garden! Which direction do your prevailing winds come from? If you're not sure, you can collect some data by putting up a windsock or just being mindful of where the wind is coming from whenever you're outside. When you check the weather, you can also take note of which direction storms move across the screen. If you live in an area with frequent strong winds, you might consider planting a windbreak. (More on this in chapter four.)

Proximity

A garden's needs are not easily forgotten when you must pass by it multiple times a day. If part of your purpose and mission is to be cooking with a lot of what you grow, make the trip between the garden and the kitchen an easy one, and it will be a trip you make more frequently.

Determine how far you will have to walk to where your tools are stored. Also, consider how accessible potential garden sites are for vehicles to drop off bulk supplies, such as soil, mulch, and compost, so you won't have to transport them by hand over a long distance.

Microclimates

A microclimate is a place that has a noticeable—but sometimes subtle—difference in conditions from the area around it. Identify any microclimates on your land. This might be a place where snow lingers in the spring or where you see the glisten of first frosts in the fall. Do certain areas get baked to a crisp in the heat of the summer? Certain microclimates might help some plants but hurt others.

Slope & Aspect

While it's certainly possible to garden on a slope, it is not without challenges. If you live in an area that gets a lot of rain, you'll likely need special management strategies to mitigate

EMBRACE YOUR GARDENING SPACE #3

Tomten Farm is an off-grid, high-altitude, educational market farm in the San Juan Mountains of Colorado. On an east-facing slope, with a clear view to the south, and blue skies for a remarkable number of days per year, ample sunlight reaches every part of the farm. Up high on a mostly open mesa, there is almost always a breeze, and the weather can change instantly. The high altitude gave us the advantage of being able to grow cool-weather crops, such as kale, spinach, arugula, and salad mix, all season long. However, outside of the greenhouse and geodesic growing dome, we never had the reliably warm weather and long frost-free season that tomatoes, peppers, melons, and many other garden favorites needed to survive and thrive. Also, water was scarce and had to be carefully managed.

THE IMPORTANCE OF OBSERVING

During a farming conference workshop session, I listened to the presenter tell a story about an urban rooftop greenhouse project. From permitting, raising money, sourcing materials, and on through to construction, tremendous efforts were made to bring the project to fruition.

Once the greenhouse started being used, however, it was clear that something wasn't working quite right. Due to the combination of shadows cast from surrounding buildings, not enough sunlight was reaching the greenhouse, particularly at the most critical times of the year.

Quite literally, not enough angles had been considered. Because not enough data had been collected, the success of the project was undermined. The greenhouse wasn't able to fulfill its original purpose of abundant year-round food production, at least not without an additional investment in a whole lot of grow lights. While it can take some time to become familiar with how the elements interact with our space throughout the seasons, it can be the difference between a garden that thrives and a garden that doesn't.

erosion when gardening on a slope. A flat space, or one that slopes only slightly, will be the easiest to work with.

Should you have the opportunity to garden on a slight slope, one facing the direction of your greatest sun exposure is ideal (unless you're trying to create a cooler or slightly less sunny microclimate). Here in the Northern Hemisphere, we get southern exposure: the south side of a building or a slope will always get more sun than the north side, and this creates a warmer, sunnier microclimate. If you have the option to choose a garden site that faces south, southeast, or southwest, it will stay a little warmer than the areas that face north. If you live in the Southern Hemisphere, the reverse is true.

Growing Zones & Frost Dates

Knowing which plant hardiness zone you live in and consulting with your local agricultural extension offices, will help you learn about what plants to grow well in your region. For more information, see the resources section at the back of the book.

The most reliable way to identify your frost-free dates is by talking with local gardeners, vegetable farmers, or staff at a nearby plant nursery. However, be aware that microclimates can exist within your region and even within the boundaries of your own space, which may affect your frost-free dates by up to a week or two.

RECOMMENDED READING FOR GARDENING FAMILIES

Sharing Nature: Nature Awareness Activities for All Ages, by Joseph Cornell, is an excellent guide to observing, experiencing, and appreciating nature in fun and creative ways. It's a must-have book for any family looking to connect more deeply with the natural world.

ACTIVITIES

MAPPING A SPACE

In his book *Mapmaking with Children*, David Sobel writes, "Maps are the clothespins that hitch our lives to our places." I love this. Making a map of your land together is a great way to create a visual key of the observations you make about your space.

First, we're going to practice mapping an indoor space. If you're already very comfortable in outdoor spaces, read through Part I to get an idea of the activity, and then skip ahead to the outdoor mapping in Part II.

You will need:

- ☐ A pencil
- ☐ Your garden journal
- ☐ A ruler (optional)
- ☐ A cushion to sit on (also optional)

Part I: Indoors: Room Map

1. Create a comfortable "sit spot" in the doorway of a room in your living space where you can observe your surroundings.

2. In your journal, draw a rough map of the room (avoid trying to make it perfect!). Include where important structures and items are in relation to each other.

3. Add labels to the different structures and then give your map a descriptive title.

4. On a separate journal page, jot down notes about the room's special features and structures: What are they? What are

their jobs? How do they work together (e.g., a light switch and a ceiling light work together to perform an important function)?

Part II: Outdoors: Through the Seasons

1. Use Google Earth (or a similar digital mapping app) to look at your space from a bird's-eye view to help you sketch out a basic outline for your land area map.

2. Choose a few different areas that you would like to observe more closely.

3. Quietly sit outside with Little Gardener. Use all five senses to carefully observe everything around you. (Spend time doing this on a seasonal basis, at varied times of day, and in diverse weather conditions.)

4. Use the following questions as guidelines for your observations and record your discoveries in your journals:

   - If you were a plant, would you be happy growing in this spot? Why or why not?
   - Is this area wet? Dry?
   - Is it exposed to the elements or more sheltered and protected?
   - What about each spot makes it a better or worse place for plants to grow?

5. Add your "gardener's eyes" observations to your land area map. (Consider showing Little Gardener how to use map symbols and create a key or a legend.)

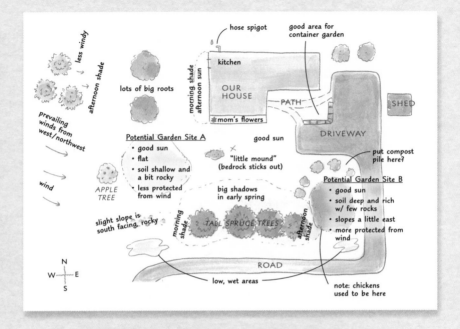

Map labels:
- less windy
- afternoon shade
- hose spigot
- good area for container garden
- kitchen
- morning shade / afternoon sun
- OUR HOUSE
- lots of big roots
- prevailing winds from west/northwest
- mom's flowers
- PATH
- SHED
- wind
- APPLE TREE
- Potential Garden Site A
  - good sun
  - flat
  - soil shallow and a bit rocky
  - less protected from wind
- good sun
- DRIVEWAY
- "little mound" (bedrock sticks out)
- put compost pile here?
- big shadows in early spring
- Potential Garden Site B
  - good sun
  - soil deep and rich w/ few rocks
  - slopes a little east
  - more protected from wind
- slight slope is south facing, rocky
- morning shade
- TALL SPRUCE TREES
- afternoon shade
- N W E S
- ROAD
- low, wet areas
- note: chickens used to be here

6. Note the best sites for a garden on your map. Where does it feel like the garden will "fit" best given what you've imagined and based on your garden's mission statement?

IDENTIFYING MICROCLIMATES

Remember that microclimates are spaces with different environmental conditions than the surrounding area—and they can exist indoors and outdoors!

Look closely at the maps you created in the prior activity and follow the directions below.

In the room that you mapped, identify any possible microclimates (e.g., the area around an AC, or sunny spot by a window). Discuss with Little Gardener how microclimates effect what kinds of activities can happen in that space.

In the outdoor space that you mapped, identify any possible microclimates. With Little Gardener, discuss how microclimates effect what activities can happen in that space.

Extra Credit

Reach out to neighbors with gardens, to local farmers and gardening clubs, or to your local agricultural extension office to locate gardens in your area you may be able to visit. When you meet with other gardeners, bring your journals for gathering ideas and helpful hints for your garden.

JOURNAL PROMPTS

- What did you observe about your outdoor space that you hadn't noticed before?
- What is the most interesting thing you noticed?
- Which observations do you think will be most helpful to you in choosing where your garden will grow?
- Has your relationship with your space changed? If so, how?

CHAPTER REVIEW

- Gardening is a powerful way to directly connect with the ecological systems that sustain us—make your garden something to celebrate.

- Use your "gardener's eyes" to help you pinpoint the site where your garden is most likely to thrive.

- Each garden site will have its distinct benefits and challenges—embrace the uniqueness of your space!

IN THE NEXT CHAPTER...

Mindfully observing your space is the most important thing you can do to choose the best spot for your garden—the information you've gathered will help you bring your dream garden into reality in your unique space. The next essential steps are identifying your specific garden goals and defining key principles that will help you achieve those goals. You're about to make some important (and fun!) decisions that will guide you closer to the garden of your dreams.

CHAPTER THREE
PREPARING

Refine your garden vision

Steam rose from the cauldron of maple sap, boiling above the fire we had built in the middle of the sugar bush. It was almost spring, but the nights were still cold, below freezing. The days were warmer and sunnier, and the trees were beginning to wake up. And while it wasn't time yet for leaf buds to be opening, the sap, the lifeblood of the tree, had begun to flow.

Three years before I met the Learning Garden, I worked as an educator at Taconic Outdoor Education Center in Clarence Fahnestock Memorial State Park in Cold Spring, New York. On Maple Sunday—an annual holiday at the center—visitors come from hours away to see the sugar shack in action, taste sap and syrup, and enjoy a syrupy breakfast. When it's not sugaring season, school and youth groups visit throughout the academic year and learn about aquatic ecology, forest ecology, animal tracking, raptors, reptiles, and how to work as a team on the Project Adventure ropes course.

In the survival skills program, students try their hands at (and test their patience with) creating fire using hand-hewn bow drills and crafting shelters with materials they find and harvest from the forest. Through tapping maple trees, collecting sap, and boiling it down to syrup, students see something delicious result from working with nature. Of all of the educational experiences we offered to help children connect with nature, this one felt the most significant to me.

On that particular Sunday, as gallons of water evaporated from the sap becoming syrup, I began to clarify my specific goals and guiding principles as it related to outdoor education and my dream of cultivating nature's keepers through fostering conscious connections to the natural world.

Pure and alive, sugar maple sap nourished a part of me that had never been attended to. I realized then that the best way to connect with nature is to eat it. And *everyone* eats.

Acknowledging this very simple fact changed the way I thought about environmental education. I built my first garden—a single raised bed—and began using it as a teaching tool at the education center. Then, I reached out to an organic farm in the Catskill Mountains to see if I could volunteer for a couple days and get a taste of what organic farming was all about. I loved it. And I ate well.

Thereafter, on different farms and homesteads, my love for growing food and cocreating with nature grew stronger through living close to the land in ways I couldn't have imagined. We

RECOMMENDED READING FOR LITTLE GARDENER

If Little Gardener would like to hear a story about how maple syrup is made from the sap of the maple tree, *Sugaring Time* by Kathryn Lasky is a great one. Interested in seeing maple sugaring up close? Every year in early spring, wherever sugar maple trees grow, you'll find maple sugaring events in action, where families can learn firsthand about how syrup is made.

SUGARING TIME

ground wheat berries to make flour for homemade bread, and split the firewood that we'd burn to bake it. We tended a tall, rainbow-colored patch of quinoa against a backdrop of snow-covered peaks. We milked goats and made fresh goat cheese. And we enjoyed countless meals outside, on the land the ingredients were grown, with friends who helped grow them. I had never felt so healthy, so awake, so alive. I felt compelled to devote my time to crafting learning experiences where young people had the opportunity to reconnect with nature the way I had.

After a few growing seasons out west on Tomten Farm, I felt called to return home to the Northeast and, several months later, found myself meeting the Learning Garden, still under the snow, for the very first time. Working with The Sylvia Center and in the Learning Garden gave me the opportunity to support their mission as well as my own newly clarified goals.

THE LEARNING GARDEN: GOALS & GUIDING LIGHTS

Recall that within the comprehensive mission of The Sylvia Center, the Learning Garden's specific mission is to provide young people with memorable experiences with fresh, healthy food, and to connect them with where it comes from and how it grows. Grateful to be given the creative license to reenvision the Learning Garden as I saw fit, I imagined a place of unforgettable food experiences, where children and families could connect with the source of their food. It would invite you in, not as a guest, but as if you had always belonged there, your connection to the life and cycles of the garden undeniably evident. It would be diverse, beautiful, abundant, peaceful, adventurous, quiet, magical, playful, in harmony with nature, and a space that cultivated wonder and was nontoxic to humans and other creatures. The garden would spark the "WOW factor," inspiring and encouraging people to try new things. The garden would be a place where the walls between people and nature would fade through engaging with the story of food from seed to plate.

Having an established mission statement for the Learning Garden made it easy to define specific goals. The Learning Garden would do the following:

> *Maintain the greatest possible diversity of colors, shapes, textures, tastes, fragrances, and plant types for Little Gardeners to explore and experience*
>
> *Have something available to pick, taste, and cook with at every point during the growing season*
>
> *Offer a variety of hands-on projects in which to participate*

Given my observations of the land and garden area, I had to ask myself if they were capable of supporting these goals. I knew there would be plenty of space to plant a diversity of vegetables, flowers, and herbs so that at any point during the growing season there would be things to harvest; the timing would need to be just right, but it could be done. Sunshine would never be a limiting factor.

The soil needed some structural work and fertility management, but the pH was in the right range for most vegetables, so we were good in that category. Water systems were not ideal in the beginning, but with a few extra watering cans, it would be workable. (My own romantic notions of watering cans hadn't yet worn off, but the time was near.) The growing season and frost dates were the most generous I'd ever had to work with—no concerns there.

I'd dreamed of a garden design that included magical, winding steps leading up to some secret water feature, like a fountain, but the flat space wasn't going to support that idea. In every space, however, there are opportunities to create magic, and I planned on seeking them out.

JUST FOR LITTLE GARDENER
IMAGINE SUCCESS

What is your number one goal for your garden? Start out with something simple like "I will grow two flowers that feed bees" or "I will grow the most delicious strawberries." Write it down in your journal. Write a story about your goal or draw a picture of yourself accomplishing it.

My knowledge of the land and the values of The Sylvia Center informed how I was going to achieve these specific goals in the garden. One of The Sylvia Center's foundational values is to help young people understand that they are "capable of making healthy food choices for themselves so that they may lead healthy and productive lives," giving them the agency to contribute to their own well-being.

I asked myself, "What guiding principles can I establish and employ to bring life back to the garden in a way that aligns with these values and objectives?" I decided to base my approach on the following principles (in no particular order):

Prioritize plant diversity

Promote play and exploration

Utilize methods and tools accessible to the average person and maximize human engagement in tending the garden

Integrate sustainable growing practices

Work with nature, not against it

Grow organically

CLARIFYING YOUR GOALS & GUIDING LIGHTS

Early spring is marked by the sun's return and is the season that lights me up the most. Everything is waking up, and there is a distinct clarity of purpose and sense of ambition that comes with that, especially when you are a gardener. Early spring is a kind of annual sunrise; no matter which garden I've been creating, working in, and caretaking, I wait patiently for this moment each year. And on that once-a-year morning, just as the lands we each steward seem to be opening their eyes, we have the opportunity to begin anew. It's time to connect more deeply with your purpose and dreams for your garden, review the observations you've made, clarify your specific goals, and identify your approach to achieving them.

Creating additional structure for your mission statement can go a long way in bringing your dream garden to life.

Remember, your mission statement explains what you are trying to accomplish by having a garden. Goals are more specific objectives you'd like to achieve. In other words, your mission informs your particular goals. Your values inform your approach to achieving them.

Take a moment to go outside and sit near where you hope your garden will grow. Reflect on the mission statement you developed in the first chapter. Given the observations you've made about the land, has anything become clearer to you regarding what your garden might be like or how you will go about creating it?

Does the order of long, clean, straight rows appeal to you? Or does the beautiful chaos of nature (with its own hidden order) offer more to invite you in? Ask yourself which approaches to gardening feel right for you and what feels like the best fit for your space. Think about your values and how they will guide you to accomplishing your goals.

WHAT ARE GROWING PRACTICES?

Growing practices are the methods you use to take care of your garden, and can also include philosophies about how to grow food. In exploring your interest in growing food, you have likely encountered terms like *organic, conventional,* and *biodynamic.* Perhaps you've heard of *no-till gardening, permaculture,* and *regenerative agriculture.* These are only a few of a myriad of approaches, and they are not mutually exclusive.

Having a basic understanding of these methods and philosophies can give you a starting point for clarifying the growing practices that align with your values. If you are particularly interested in gardening with nature's rhythms and cycles, you may want to learn more about biodynamic growing practices. If you value supporting the soil food web, you may be interested in no-till gardening.

CHECKING IN WITH YOUR ENVIRONMENT

Revisit the site observations you made in chapter two (see page 44). Are your goals compatible with what your space and environmental conditions can support? Are they reasonably practical?

If you live in a climate like that of Tomten Farm (very short growing season, unpredictable summer temperatures), growing tomatoes and hot peppers for your salsa will be a tall order without a greenhouse or some small structure that could provide a warmer and more protected microclimate.

You may have dreamed of growing sweet potatoes to make your own chips, or bananas to go on your morning granola, but your North Dakota winters won't support it without a greenhouse, artificial lights, and additional heat inputs. Is enough sunlight reaching your porch to support growing the four different kinds of basil you're hoping to grow in your container garden?

Tulsi Basil
(Holy Basil)

Red Rubin
Basil

Lemon/Lime
Basil

Cinnamon
Basil

ACTIVITIES

YOUR GARDEN VISION

Part I: Setting Goals

In your journals, take a few minutes to review your mission statement. Then identify your specific goals about what you would like to grow, learn, achieve, or experience.

Here are some examples to help you create goals using your mission statement:

Mission statement:
Our garden grows fresh food to nourish our family.

Possible goals (one or more):

- We will have at least one ingredient ready to harvest weekly from the garden.

- We will grow ingredients to make our own fresh salsa.

- We will grow herbs that we can add to our iced tea on hot summer days.

Mission statement:
As we cultivate fresh fruits, vegetables, and flowers, our garden will be a place where we can explore plant life cycles and study relationships between insects and the garden.

Possible goals (one or more):

- Each week, we will draw pictures in our journal to illustrate how plants change through the growing season.

- We will spend time in the garden each week and record observations of insects and which plants they visit.

Part II: Identifying Your Guiding Lights

Review the gardening values you identified in chapter one (see page 23).

What guidelines would you like to establish that will help you create and manage your garden in alignment with those values?

Identify at least three guiding principles that embody your values and record them in your journal. Here are some examples:

- If you value "creating safe spaces for endangered pollinators," you can commit to not using pesticides of any kind.

- If you value "connecting to the soil," you can use fewer mechanized tools in favor of your hands and hand tools.

- If you value "providing an abundance of food for my family," you can choose to plant intensively to produce as much food as possible in the space you have.

KEEPING YOUR VISION & GOALS ALIVE

Staying focused on your mission, particularly throughout the growing season, can be challenging. We all have experienced the way New Year's resolution ambitions fade over time; losing track of our goals happens to the best of us. You've already done the hard work of clarifying what you'd like to do; now how will you stay connected to manifesting your vision and accomplishing your mission?

To help myself stay focused, I like to write down my mission statement, goals, and guiding principles (all together, in one place) on the inside cover of my garden journal, where it's easy to find. Here is an example:

Mission (What):
Reconnect with nature and grow food in a way that honors and supports other life.

Goals (Specifically What):
Spend 20 minutes each week in silent observation of life in the garden. Cultivate bee-friendly flowers.

Guiding Principles (How):
Use our own hands rather than machines to do garden work. Avoid using pesticides and herbicides, which may hurt pollinators and damage their habitats.

Then I'll post my mission statement in a place where I know I will see it every day. Your reminder could be as simple as a sticky note on the fridge or as grand as a banner above your kitchen window. You and Little Gardener can create one "reminder" together or each create your own expression of your shared mission—use words, draw pictures, or make a collage—whatever comes naturally.

Think of your creation as a part of your garden that lives inside your house, a friendly reminder of what you intend to cocreate outdoors with nature.

THE MAGIC OF "SO THAT" STATEMENTS

One way I love to clarify my path forward on any big project is to create a string of "so that" statements in my journal. This helps me organize my thoughts and clarify tasks I need to do to achieve my desired outcome.

I begin my list with a solid, clear goal, and work backward toward a purpose, the all-important reminder of why I'm doing what I'm doing.

Example:

I will write a book about gardening for Big Gardeners and Little Gardeners

so that...

families can create a garden together

so that...

they can have direct experiences with nature and where their food comes from

so that...

Big Gardeners and Little Gardeners realize that food is nature

so that...

they know that natural systems support their well-being

so that...

humans will take better care of the natural systems that sustain them and all other life.

In your journal, make your own "so that" list about your garden and then guide Little Gardener through the activity.

Note: If Little Gardener is very little, work together in conversation to create a few very simple "so that" statements. For example: "We will grow a lot of flowers *so that* bees and butterflies have food."

JOURNAL PROMPTS

- Why is it important to check in with ourselves as well as our environment when we are planning a garden?
- What do you think it means to consider both what you want and what the land "wants"?

CHAPTER REVIEW

- The best way to connect with nature is to eat it. And *everyone* eats.

- Creating a mission statement, goals, and guiding principles can go a long way in bringing your dream garden to life.

- Check in with your environment—be sure your garden goals are reasonably practical given your unique site.

IN THE NEXT CHAPTER...

Building a strong foundation for any project begins with taking the time to set intentions. Crafting your garden to meet those intentions may be the most exciting part of the journey—you'll see your garden dreams begin to manifest. The next step in designing a garden that works well with your unique environment is recognizing your garden as an ecosystem. There are specific garden features that can help generate abundance, promote easy maintenance, and encourage play and engagement.

CRAFTING YOUR GARDEN

CHAPTER FOUR
DESIGNING

Shape the garden to your intentions
and environment

"See that bathtub over there?" I whispered to the small group of Little Gardeners. Slowly, and with as much wonder and magic as I could muster, I said, "You can *eat* any flower you find growing in that bathtub."

"You're allowed to eat flowers? You just blew my mind!" said nine-year-old Carter.

The antique tub had found new life in the Learning Garden as our edible-flower bathtub. Unusual, eye-catching, and overflowing with multicolored flowers, the tub drew students toward it. Its unmistakable borders clearly defined a space where flowers were safe to eat. Little Gardeners could have total freedom in deciding which ones they wanted to try, without needing explicit permission from a grown-up.

On a garden tour, whenever students' focus and interest waned, edible flowers were my saving grace. I would discreetly start picking and eating them until a student noticed and asked, often with a degree of alarm, what exactly it was that I was doing. "Eating flowers," I'd respond nonchalantly, which would elicit the quiet focus and surprised wide eyes I was hoping for. Eating something they'd never thought of as food awakened their natural curiosity and prompted questions about what other parts of nature were edible.

The edible-flower bathtub met several of my goals for the Learning Garden. It was a magical garden space with a diversity of plants that supported pollinators. Little Gardeners were awestruck by edible nature and became self-directed learners as they engaged with the garden in their own way.

In your garden, what structures and design elements will you create to meet your goals? How can each of those features serve several purposes?

The next step in designing a garden is deciding on its layout and the shapes of some of its parts. It's time to think about how different parts of the garden (including you) will work together and how you will create a garden ecosystem that's a fit for the land it is on.

DESIGNING A GARDEN
THAT MIMICS NATURE

While a garden ecosystem is a far cry from the richness of wild, uncultivated ecosystems, gardens can be designed and planned in a way that resembles natural systems—and supports many more ecological relationships than a traditional lawn. An effective garden design considers the unique conditions and limiting factors of space, time, climate, soil, weather, energy, money, and infrastructure and how different components of the system will work together.

Webs of diverse, integrated relationships between living things and their environment create resilient ecosystems, and in cultivated ecosystems like gardens, everything is connected too—each member and element of the system contributes to the ecosystem in multiple ways. While these cultivated systems can be challenging to maintain, they are less so when your

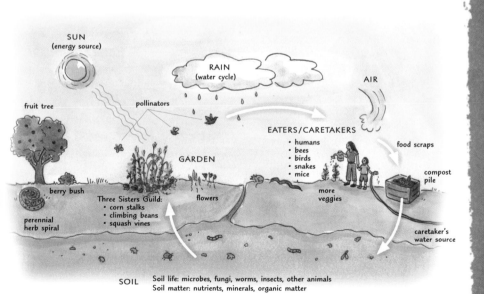

SUN
(energy source)

RAIN
(water cycle)

AIR

fruit tree

pollinators

EATERS/CARETAKERS
• humans
• bees
• birds
• snakes
• mice

food scraps

GARDEN

compost pile

berry bush

Three Sisters Guild:
• corn stalks
• climbing beans
• squash vines

flowers

more veggies

perennial herb spiral

caretaker's water source

SOIL   Soil life: microbes, fungi, worms, insects, other animals
Soil matter: nutrients, minerals, organic matter

design and plans mimic systems that are already working well in nature. The more webs of connection there are, the healthier your garden ecosystem will be.

When we use natural ecosystems as models for our garden ecosystems, we not only create abundance for ourselves but for other creatures as well. One way to do this is by creating habitats in your garden for creatures such as garter snakes and toads—an offering of free room and board. Thousands of insects can be devoured by a single toad over the course of a summer, and snakes will be more than grateful to assist with managing rodent and slug populations, which you, as the gardener, would otherwise have to negotiate. Garter snakes and toads are designed to "deal with" these issues, so why not let them? (If you have any reservations about inviting these creatures to the party, just know that rodents and slugs both love strawberries. And I'm guessing you do too.)

TEAMWORK IN ECOSYSTEMS

The term *symbiosis* describes a close relationship between two different species. Familiar to most gardeners is the partnership that exists between legumes (like peas and beans) and bacteria that live on their roots; the bacteria harvest nitrogen from the air and make it available for plants to use.

Fungi and plants are longtime friends too. Special fungi (called *mycorrhizae*) attach to a plant's roots, creating a pathway for the plant and fungi to work together. The plant shares some of the energy it produces from the sun, and the fungus allows the plant to take up additional nutrients and water and protects the plants from diseases. These relationships are called *mycorrhizal associations* and I find them to be *the* most fascinating element of ecology.

A LEARNING GARDEN DESIGNED
FOR LITTLE GARDENERS

The goals of the growing spaces at The Sylvia Center, Tomten Farm, and Wyomanock Farm are to support a blend of educational, inspirational, ecological, and sustainable abundance objectives. The structure and layout of the Learning Garden enabled us to meet those objectives and make the dream of the garden come alive.

When the Learning Garden came under my care, seven grassy curved paths were already established. The garden beds formed a beautifully imperfect south-facing rainbow that measured about one hundred feet wide across its base, and slightly more than one hundred feet from top to bottom. The curves were a fun alternative to straight rows, inviting Little Gardeners to explore what was just around the bend.

Inside the innermost arc of the rainbow, near the garden's entrance, we planted the highest concentration of flowers and herbs. Among the flower and herb beds were grassy spaces to gather Little Gardeners and welcome them to the garden. In this space, we could seamlessly transition from introducing the garden to touching, smelling, and tasting the nearby herbs, which children generally found to be less intimidating as a starting point than taking a bite of asparagus.

Some herbs were grown in herb spirals, a special design that creates microclimates of temperature and moisture. The "bed" is mound-shaped with a miniature retaining wall of rocks spiraling from bottom to top to help keep the soil in place and define an attractive edge. Different sides of the mound receive different amounts of light and warm up at different rates throughout the day, and the top of the mound has better drainage than the bottom part. Herb spirals allowed us to create microclimates customized for certain plants based on how warm or moist they preferred to be.

Surrounded by fragrant lemon balm, strawberries, and edible flowers, another bathtub had been repurposed as a water feature. The small solar panel beside it powered an electric water pump that created a little fountain in the middle of the water-filled tub. Hearing the sound of water flowing changed the dynamic of the garden experience (and brought peace of mind to tired gardeners at the end of many long, hot days).

The Learning Garden featured a diversity of colors, textures, and flavors that changed throughout the season. At the peak of the growing season, Little Gardeners both short and tall had access to plants growing at varied heights, from strawberries and herbs at ground level to trellised tomatoes more than five feet tall, and flower blooms beaming out at every height in between. Winding through the area underneath the rainbow was a tunnel-shaped trellis that, covered with the vines and leaves of scarlet runner beans and Malabar spinach, Little Gardeners could crawl through and hide under.

Facing south and lining the outermost arc of the rainbow, multicolored sunflowers four times the size of our littlest Little Gardeners hugged the garden. A beautifully carved wooden sculpture shaped like a happy mouth greeted Little Gardeners at the entrance, encouraging them to try new foods. Features like these helped us create the "wow" moments that made the Learning Garden a place of magic, meaning, and inspiration.

Making Adjustments

Every season, we learned how the space could better serve Little Gardeners and then tweaked the Learning Garden's design. We found that the paths were not quite wide enough for larger groups to move through without stepping on the beds, and in some places the boundary between bed and path was not distinct enough for Little Gardeners to know where it was safe to walk. The beds themselves were sometimes too wide for Big Gardeners to jump over (especially while carrying garden tools) and too wide for Little Gardeners to reach the middle of.

While the curved paths encouraged exploration, they also presented maintenance challenges. Operating our cumbersome lawnmower on the curved paths was an unwelcome task. On beds that needed protection from cold snaps, insects, and groundhogs, it was tough to get the long, straight pieces of row cover to sit just right and stay that way.

Improvements came with every new season. We lined the edges of the main path with marigolds, and the bright yellow flowers acted like the lights you see along the floor of a movie theater or airplane aisle. Eventually, long, curved beds were broken up into smaller ones, allowing us to create additional paths that facilitated travel between different arcs of the rainbow and made keeping the beds covered much easier.

Eventually, a tall fence was built to protect the whole farm from deer. Far from the garden and hidden out of sight by trees at the field's edge, the fence protected the garden without making it feel exclusive.

GARDEN LAYOUT & STRUCTURE—THE BASICS

Natural systems are complex; in crafting a garden, it's up to you to decide how far down the rabbit hole you'd like to go.

Most of us would probably love to have a big garden that is diverse, abundant, beautiful, accessible, easy to maintain, resilient, and ecologically regenerative. We'd love it to have clean soil with perfect texture and drainage, and just the right amount of sun, magic, and intrigue.

You can spend as much or as little time as you like designing your garden to make it the best that it can be. Be mindful too that while it's great to dream big, it's good to start small. (Once you've been working with your garden for a year or two, you'll know whether you can handle managing additional growing space.)

Choosing the shape of your garden and designing its beds and paths is one of the most exciting parts of the design process.

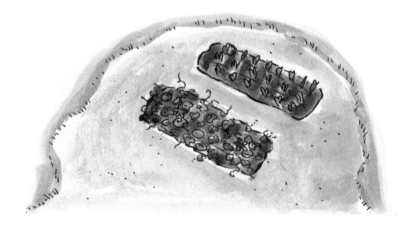

CONTAINER GARDENS

If you're short on space, or are interested in growing just a few things, consider planting a container garden. It is just what it sounds like: growing plants in whatever kinds of containers are available to you. Garden pots, recycled milk jugs, hanging baskets, and five-gallon pails can all serve as beautiful, creative, and abundant growing spaces. To save more space, you might consider going vertical, focusing your efforts on growing plants that are natural climbers (pole beans and peas) or those that can be trained to climb (cucumbers and tomatoes).

If you're short on time, container gardens help keep the area you need to focus on small, simple, and more manageable too. (Learn how to make your own container garden in chapter six on page 135.)

Here are some steps you can take to start clarifying the shapes and borders you'd like to include in your garden layout:

- Walk your garden site. What shape would you like the exterior edge of your garden to be? A square? A rectangle? A circle? Or some irregular shape you dream up yourself?

- Consider any limitations of time, money, and resources, and reconnect with the goals you clarified in chapter three. What layout best aligns with your goals?

- Reflect on how you will accommodate the different functions that your garden needs to perform. How much of your site do you want for growing space and how much for walkways and places to relax and play?

Beds

What shape will your garden beds be? While square or rectangular beds tend to be more manageable when it comes to building and planning, a garden with curves can feel more natural and magical than being surrounded by ninety-degree angles.

To keep the garden user-friendly, bed width should be no longer than twice your comfortable reach from a kneeling position. For most Big Gardeners, a bed width of four feet is workable, though three feet may be more comfortable. Beds specifically designed for Little Gardeners should be no more three feet wide, and for Tiny Gardeners, no more than two feet wide.

Raised Beds

Raised beds are growing spaces made to sit higher than ground level and can range from a few inches to a few feet deep. They may be contained by constructed borders or may simply be soil that is raked and maintained to the desired height. Growing in beds at ground level is certainly an option. If you talk to any group of gardeners, however, you'll often find a shared fondness for raised beds as their advantages are numerous.

In springtime, the soil in raised beds warms up faster, giving gardeners a head start on the growing season—the beds are microclimates! They are also easy to work in, have better drainage, and their soil is less likely to be stepped on and compacted, which adversely affects plant growth. If you have contaminated, shallow, rocky, or otherwise less-than-ideal soil, raised beds offer an opportunity to a create new growing space with improved soil conditions.

The icing on the cake is that they are uncomplicated to build and easy to customize to your needs. For example, extra-tall raised beds can be crafted for gardeners who have trouble reaching down to the ground. With extra time and dedication, even curved raised beds are possible!

Paths

Paths should be wide enough to comfortably allow you and Little Gardener to move supplies with a wheelbarrow, a wagon, a bucket in each hand, or your preferred method of transport. Make sure there is enough space to kneel between the beds in a way that is comfortable for you, and to push your mower through if you'll have grassy paths—think joyful maintenance!

If you have alter-abled friends, family members with limited mobility, wild children, or anyone who might benefit from having extra space to move about in the garden, keep your paths nice and wide. In the Learning Garden, our paths eventually grew to almost five feet wide to be sure gardeners of all abilities (and energy levels) had access to the garden.

Fences

Some gardeners will say that you absolutely must have a fence. I believe a more reasonable response to the fence question is "It depends." It depends on where you live, what your goals are, and who or what you are trying to keep out. In my opinion, fenceless spaces are infinitely more inviting, and I've had some decent luck without a fence.

Certain plants just aren't of real interest to the medium- and large-size animals that a fence is erected to keep out. Rhubarb, potatoes, anything in the onion family (onions, garlic, shallots, leeks, chives), and very aromatic herbs, such as rosemary, thyme, oregano, mint, sage, and lavender, all tend to be left alone. If fenced space is a limiting factor, don't waste it on these plants.

Sometimes You Need a Giant Fence
At Tomten Farm, a seven- or eight-foot-high page-wire fence with large wooden fence posts kept the deer and elk out (as long as we remembered to close the gate), and a fence of similar height around the entire Katchkie Farm property protected the much smaller Learning Garden. Prior to the fence being built, the deer once wiped out thousands of lettuce plants on the farm in a single night. The fence helped with the deer pressure, but the groundhogs regularly had us outnumbered.

Sometimes You Just Get Lucky
On Wyomanock Farm, our half-acre garden of mixed vegetables and flowers was not fenced in. Unwanted trespassers included rogue chickens, an occasional escapee from the cattle herd, or, even rarer, a rabbit or groundhog. Canadian geese would eat the leaves of our corn seedlings, and mice would often leave tooth marks in our beets, but these were not issues a fence would have addressed.

I've noticed that the farther a garden is from the forest's edge, the fewer wild creatures find their way in. This garden was basically in the middle of an open field. Perhaps animals,

such as rabbits, were not willing to risk being so far from the protection of the forest. Maybe it was the scent of our dog or the presence of the cattle. How we were lucky enough to avoid pressure from deer and other mammals I don't know, but I was always grateful for whatever deterrent, invisible to me, kept the vegetables safe.

EXPLORING OTHER DESIGN FEATURES & HELPFUL STRUCTURES

After deciding on the basic infrastructure of your garden—its general shape, layout, and types of beds and paths—it's time to dive into the next layer of design.

Explore the following features and structures that can help integrate your garden into natural systems and support bringing your garden dream to life.

Keyhole Gardens

I believe you'll become fast friends with keyhole gardens. Unique, beautiful, efficient, and inviting, this is an ingenious design concept that can be used with raised or ground-level beds.

Imagine you and Little Gardener sitting in the middle of a path in your garden, and fifteen different things to eat are within arm's reach. This would be an unlikely circumstance in most traditional garden designs, where long straight beds waste precious growing space on paths.

Keyhole designs maximize growing space by getting creative with the size and shape of the bed and path. Visualize taking a bed four feet wide by fifteen feet long and bending it into a horseshoe shape so that the ends almost touch, and you'll see that a keyhole shape remains as the path. Sitting right in the center of your keyhole, you can literally surround yourself with your garden. (See page 91.)

Creating Microclimates with Sun-Traps & Windbreaks

Sun-traps are a design feature that you can use to create warmer microclimates in your garden. Shaped like a U, sun-traps open to face the direction of greatest sun exposure (south if you're in the Northern Hemisphere and north if you're in the Southern Hemisphere). Taller, more robust plants hug the outer edge of the U, "trap" the heat energy from the sunlight, and radiate it inward toward smaller, more heat-loving plants. Sun-traps work well with the curved shape of keyhole gardens.

If you live in a windy place, a windbreak of taller plantings can create a protected microclimate that mitigates wind erosion, the loss of soil moisture to evaporation, and the effects of strong wind on tender plants. To maximize the collective benefit of keyhole gardens and windbreaks, face the keyhole entrance away from prevailing winds, and let your taller plantings hug the perimeter on the windy side.

Do you have any existing structures, like a stone wall, that could serve as a sun-trap? Or a row of bushes that could serve as a windbreak?

HAVING A GAME PLAN FOR WATERING

Unless you are designing an extensive garden space, there's no need to install a complicated irrigation system—a hose and watering wand, a sprinkler, or soaker hoses will suffice. Simply make sure you have convenient access to water and that your design accommodates your watering methods. After you have a year or two of gardening under your belt, you'll have a better understanding of your garden, climate, schedule, and what you like to grow, and you can decide if a more complex irrigation system is necessary.

Trellises & Arbors

Incorporating trellises, arbors, or pergolas into your garden design can create shady areas for humans and shade-tolerant ornamentals, provide support for climbing plants, and offer special hiding places for Little Gardeners.

A trellis is anything that a plant climbs or uses for support as it grows, while an arbor is formed by trees or climbing plants that are usually trained over a wooden framework to form a shaded, tunnel-like passageway.

Pergolas are larger versions of arbors and are strong enough to support an entire "roof" of plant growth overhead with "walls" to the sides, creating a full "room." Frames for these types of structures can be built or purchased in a variety of sizes and styles, ranging from small tepee-style trellises to large pergolas that could cover an entire patio. Utilizing vertical

HELPFUL HINT
SAVE SOME SPACE

Save a little space for any unexpected ideas that will undoubtedly come to you later in the design process. You may want to include a space for sitting or camping out, secret spaces to hide and play, or even a small table at which you could enjoy a fresh-picked meal or a cup of sun tea.

space—having greenery up, around, and over you—can give your space a wild and mystical feel.

Adult-Free Space

Embrace uncertainty by letting Little Gardener take full responsibility for a particular area of the garden. Magic can happen in garden beds where adults do not interfere. Delineating a small area with twine and stakes will do the trick.

If you prefer more structure, square-foot gardening is the way to go. Following this method, a three-foot-square raised bed is divided into nine square-foot sections or, for Tiny Gardeners, a two-foot-square bed is divided into four sections. Garden beds divided into individual equal-sized squares make it easy for Little Gardeners to plan, grow, and manage their garden bed square-by-square. (See page 91.)

(See page 91.)

HELPFUL HINT

STAYING ORGANIZED

Plan to keep your tools in a dry space that is convenient to the garden. If you plan to have a compost pile, choose a site convenient to both the garden and your kitchen (the place where compost materials presumably will be coming from). Somewhere along a well-traveled route between the two would be ideal. There will be some inevitable amount of garden clutter—extra plant labels, harvest baskets, seeding trays, bags of potting soil—so you'll want to have a plan for where this stuff will live and make sure it's easily accessible.

POSTSCRIPT

There's a lot to think about here, but don't panic. We'll be discussing many of these structures and features in greater detail in the pages to come—and, in chapter six, we'll look at how to build some of them.

ACTIVITIES

WALKING YOUR GARDEN LAYOUT

I would love for your garden to become a big and meaningful part of your life, and a thoughtful design will make this happen.

1. Review your land area map (from chapter two); focus in on the area that you think will be the best site for your garden.

2. On a separate piece of paper, draw a map of just that area. On this new map, sketch a proposed layout for your garden. (Alternatively, you can use a mapping app to print a bird's-eye view of the garden site.)

3. Go out to the garden site and play with the layout in a hands-on way. Big Gardener and Little Gardener can work together to tap in wooden stakes and connect them with twine to define the outer border.

4. Do the same as above to mark where you think your paths and beds might go.

Note: If you're starting off with a hard surface—too hard for stakes—use flour to sprinkle outlines of your garden's shapes and borders (like lines on a baseball field), or use rope or garden hoses instead. You can also get creative with props to represent special design elements (like trellises). Walk through the space together. Ask the following questions:

- Does the scale feel right for both you and Little Gardener?

- Can you comfortably reach the middle of every soon-to-be-cultivated area?

- Can you fit your wheelbarrow, or carry buckets and baskets where needed? Move a hose around the space without harming plants?

- Is there space allocated for everything you'd like your garden to be?

- Have you considered wet spots, rocky areas, or other distinct areas?

Review your mission and goals, and remind yourself how you want your garden to feel. Play with the layout more if needed and make any final adjustments to your design and then to your map.

DISCOVERING ECOSYSTEM RELATIONSHIPS

In this activity, you'll get to know the workings of the natural world even more deeply by identifying and exploring ecological relationships in both wild and cultivated nature.

You will need:

☐ Wildlife, nature, and gardening magazines, as well as seed catalogs, that you can cut up. (Ask at a local library if they have any old ones you can take off their hands.)

☐ Two corkboards
☐ Scissors
☐ Pushpins
☐ String or yarn

Part I: Exploring Relationships in Wild Nature

1. Cut pictures from the magazines of plants, animals, and environmental features (e.g., soil, ponds, streams, and tree stumps) that might exist in an ecosystem together (or draw pictures of them yourself!).

2. Using pushpins, attach them to your corkboard. What kinds of relationships or interactions exist between the members of the system?

3. When you identify a relationship, use a piece of string to visually connect the members by wrapping it around each picture's pushpin (e.g., if a fox and a mouse live in this ecosystem, you can connect them because foxes eat mice).

4. After you've made as many connections as you can, answer the following questions in your journal:

   · How many relationships did you identify?

   · What happens if you remove one of the pictures? (e.g., what might happen to the beaver if there were no more trees?)

   · If a particular relationship no longer exists, how might this affect other members or features of the system?

Part II: Exploring Relationships in Cultivated Nature

1. Follow the instructions in Part I to create a garden ecosystem using pictures of plants, animals, and environmental features that you might find in a garden. (Don't forget to include a picture of yourself in your garden ecosystem!)

2. Does everything in the garden have multiple connections? What might you add to the system to cultivate more relationships?

3. Return to your journal and revisit the questions from Part I as they pertain to your garden. How are the relationships within each of these systems—wild nature and a cultivated garden—similar to each other?

JOURNAL PROMPTS

- What else might make your garden design more effective?
- What would happen if bees were no longer part of your garden system?
- What would happen if *you* were no longer part of your garden system?

CHAPTER REVIEW

- When the design of your garden mimics a natural ecosystem, it will be more abundant, more resilient, less work, and offer valuable habitat for other creatures.

- Decide on the types of beds and paths that will shape the layout of your garden. Consider fun, creative elements like trellises, arbors, and keyhole beds.

- Physically map out your garden in real space using hoses, lengths of rope, and other props to represent design features, making sure it's a good fit for both Big Gardener and Little Gardener.

IN THE NEXT CHAPTER...

Designing your garden can be as simple or complex an undertaking as you want it to be. The same goes for planning. Creating a planting plan before the growing season begins will help you to effectively use your garden space to achieve your goals. You're about to discover that figuring out what to plant, when to plant it, how much to plant, and where it should go is a fun annual puzzle to be solved—and enjoyed.

CHAPTER FIVE

PLANNING

Set up your garden map and calendar

A small group of first and second graders followed me to a lush garden bed in the Learning Garden. We planned to harvest a few heads of lettuce for the salad we were making that day. Kneeling at the bed's edge, we looked at our choices: red butterhead, speckled romaine, and a frilly summer crisp. "Ummmm…where is all of the regular lettuce?" one student asked, a little confused.

I smiled, and explained that there's really no such thing as "regular lettuce." There are hundreds and possibly thousands of different types. I noted that just because the light-colored, crunchy iceberg variety might be the one we see most often doesn't mean it's the only kind or the best kind.

Over two hundred different varieties of vegetables, fruits, culinary and medicinal herbs, and edible and ornamental flowers grew in the Learning Garden each year. Throughout the growing season, there was always something for Little Gardeners to pick, taste, and use as an ingredient in the farm-fresh lunch we prepared together.

Unusual looking edibles were everywhere, challenging Little Gardeners' perceptions of what food looks like. Cucamelons (Mexican sour gherkins), bitesize lemony cucumbers resembling miniature watermelons; rhubarb's sour stems under their giant inedible leaves; fifteen different varieties of tomatoes of various

THREE SISTERS GUILD

In the design methodology known as *permaculture*, the word "guild" is used to describe a collection of plants that humans have grouped together based on the plants' abilities to mimic the structures and functions of a wild ecosystem.

The Three Sisters guild—corn, beans, and squash—is one of the more well-known plant guilds. This thoughtful companion planting arrangement practiced by Native Americans wisely uses the individual characteristics and habits of these plants to create a system that benefits all three, as well as the land on which they grow.

Corn is planted first, then beans (the climbing variety), then squash (wide-spreading winter varieties). The corn comes up first, providing a natural trellis for the beans.

In symbiotic partnership with beneficial bacteria that live on their roots, beans can fix nitrogen —harvesting it from the air and releasing it into the soil, where it can be used by the corn and the squash. The extensive squash vines colonize the ground, their big leaves creating shade, which minimizes the evaporation of soil moisture, keeps weeds at bay, and mitigates soil erosion.

The Rocky Mountain bee plant (*Cleome serrulata*) is considered by some to be a fourth sister. Though it does have edible parts, its most important job is to attract pollinators to the planting, making this guild even more dynamic and resilient.

flavors, shapes, and colors; husk cherries, a sweet treat wrapped in a papery case and harvested from where they fall to the ground; the intensely sugary leaves of stevia; and dozens of other bizarre and common foods could be found in every nook and cranny of the garden.

Following nature's lead, we strived to never leave soil bare. Instead, we encouraged biological activity and limited erosion by using techniques like cover cropping (see page 164) and interplanting (see page 102). An entire bed was devoted to bee- and pollinator-friendly flowers, with a birdhouse and small birdbath nestled among them. Corn, beans, and squash illustrated the well-known Three Sisters guild of plants.

Planning for the Learning Garden to be an effective teaching tool while also maintaining its beauty, abundance, and ecological health throughout the entire growing season was an awesome challenge—and one of the most fun parts about taking care of an educational garden.

In this chapter, we've arrived at another point in the process of creating a garden when the depths of another rabbit hole beckon. As you read, decide how far you'd like to sink into the details. What level of planning makes sense to you and for your space? Some of us are natural planners; others like to fly by the seat of our pants. Garden planning is a practical way to indulge your and Little Gardener's urge to problem-solve and to practice and improve those skills.

ORGANIZING YOUR GROWING SPACE

You've established the size and shape of your garden beds. Now you'll need to create an easy-to-remember name for each bed, and then divide each bed into sections on your map.

For example, if you have two square raised beds in your design, start by calling them "Left and Right" or "West and East," and divide them into sections. If you've decided to try square foot gardening, divide three-foot-square beds into nine smaller square sections, or two-foot-square beds into four smaller ones. Identify each section with a number or a letter.

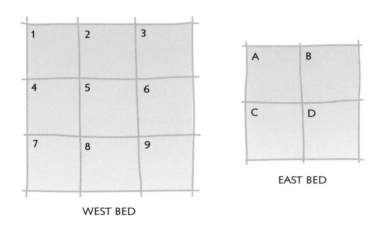

WEST BED

EAST BED

For keyhole designs, divide the bed into equal sections around the entire "doughnut," like this:

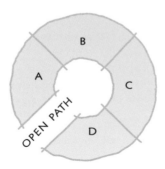

My first year managing the Learning Garden, my sketch of garden beds and planting sections looked like this:

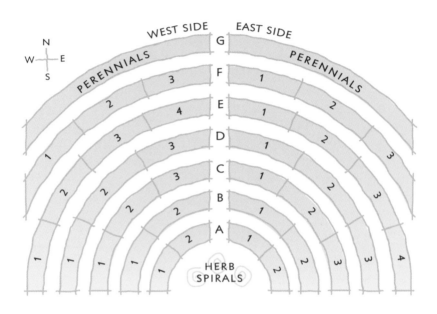

HOW TO PLAN A GARDEN

Here is a quick checklist of steps to follow when planning a garden:

☐ Create names for your garden beds and divide each bed into sections.

☐ Decide what you would like to grow.

☐ Learn more about each plant, including how it likes to be seeded, how much space it needs, and how long it will take to grow.

☐ Choose how much of each plant you would like to grow.

☐ Decide which garden bed and section each one will grow in.

WHAT, WHEN, HOW MUCH & WHERE

Planning a garden is one of the coolest puzzles you'll ever do. Guaranteed. No matter what your garden goals are, or what your affection or aptitude for planning is, figuring out the details of the season can be done in four simple, fairly painless, interconnected steps: deciding what to grow, when to grow it, how much of it to grow, and where. As you work through each of these steps, be mindful of your vision of what you want your garden to feel like.

What Should I Grow?

Around Thanksgiving, seed catalogs start coming in the mail. I leaf through them with the same kind of awe I did as an eight-year-old paging through the Sears Wish Book before Christmas. Many seed catalogs go beyond listing what seeds are available, and include specific planting instructions. Some, like Fedco, are incredibly well-written, offer stories about the unusual history of some of the varieties, and often make me laugh out loud.

Before you go on a bender of ogling seed catalogs until the sun comes up, think back to the first chapter, where you dreamed up your ideal garden. Revisit your mission statement, observations about your land,

WELCOMING BUTTERFLIES & BEES

Are you inviting bees and butterflies to find food in your garden? Support pollinators by planting an assortment of flowers and herbs that will offer blooms across the growing season. Some of my favorites are bee balm, butterfly bush, coneflower, and phacelia. (Some herbs, such as thyme and dill, not only attract pollinators and are edible, but also deter pests!) Check with your local garden center to see which varieties grow well in your area. Give preference to native plant species, which have coevolved with native insect and bird life.

and clarified goals. Recall conversations you've had with nearby gardeners or farmers about your unique regional climate and the varieties of vegetables and fruits that grow best there. Think about what you and your family love to eat or would like to try growing.

Consider aesthetics too—patterns of plant types (flowers, vegetables, herbs, fruits, shrubs), shapes, colors, heights, and textures. Choose a mix of warm- and cool-weather crops to maximize your harvest across the growing season. Remember that the greater diversity you have (polyculture plantings) the stronger your garden ecosystem will be, especially against pests and disease.

Take out your journals and work together to make a "final" list of what you would like to grow. If this is your first gardening rodeo, choosing no more than ten vegetables or fruits is a reasonable place to start. (I suggest you plant at least two or three varieties of one crop—you'll see why in chapter nine).

As you consider the timing of your plantings, where you will plant them, and how much you will plant, you may decide to narrow down your selection. Your confidence as a gardener will develop throughout the season, and eventually you'll be able to manage more.

RECOMMENDED READING FOR BIG GARDENER

Frank Tozer's *The Vegetable Growers Handbook* has been my gardening bible for the last ten years. The most user-friendly vegetable gardener's reference book I've ever come across, it clearly communicates the "vitals" (including planting ratios, germination temperatures, days to maturity, and a slew of other information) for common vegetable crops and for a few unusual ones too. I highly suggest you acquire a copy.

Getting to Know Your Plants

Collect as much of the following information as you can for each plant you would like to grow, and record it in your journal.

Direct Seed or Start Seedlings for Transplant: Does this plant prefer to be direct seeded (meaning, it will grow and mature in that very spot through the end of the season) or started indoors before being transplanted to its final place outside? Does it make more sense to start the seedlings yourselves or to purchase them from a nursery?

Annual or Perennial: Does this plant come back year after year in the specific plant hardiness zone where you live (perennial), or will it need to be replanted every year (annual)? If it is an annual, will it self-sow (drop seeds that will create new plants the following year)?

Planting Date: How long before or after your average last frost date in the spring, or first frost date in the fall, should this seed or seedling be planted?

Germination and Growing Temperature: How warm does it have to be for the seed to germinate (sprout)? In what temperature range is this plant "happy"?

Hardiness: How well does this plant tolerate frost?

Days to Maturity: How long after planting a seed or seedling will you be able to harvest it (if all goes well)?

Space: How far apart should you plant the seeds? How much space is needed for a full-grown plant to be successful? (*Note:* In areas that are very wet, plan to leave a little extra room between plants, especially if they have dense foliage. Additional space allows for increased air circulation and evaporation, both of which help mitigate disease.)

Pollination Needs: Does this plant need to be near others of its kind for pollination?

Yield: How much can you expect to harvest from a healthy plant? How many people will one plant feed? For how many weeks can you expect a yield?

When Should I Grow It?

In mid-June, students at the Learning Garden would often ask, "Are we going to eat watermelon today?" as we walked toward garden.

"What kind of weather do watermelons like to grow in?" I'd inquire.

"Summer!"

"Yes, they like warm weather. Have we had a lot of warm weather yet this year?"

"No, not yet."

"There haven't been enough warm days for watermelons to grow. In fact, we only just transplanted our watermelon seedlings outside this week, because even last week, it was still too cold for them. If you come back in August, they'll be ready to pick and eat."

RECOMMENDED READING FOR LITTLE GARDENER

Through sing-song rhyme, the children's book *What Makes the Seasons?* by Megan Montague Cash takes young readers on a journey through seasonal changes—why they happen and their effects on plant growth. The story lays the groundwork for connecting even the Littlest Gardeners to the rhythms of the planet and how gardeners use Earth's cycles to plan what we grow when.

How to Keep Track of Your Planting Schedule

Before spring sneaks up on me, I like to create a planting calendar to help me manage when to plant what. Noting important dates—including frost dates and when to seed or transplant each type of plant I want to grow—keeps me organized and helps me use my garden space (and my time) efficiently. This results, ideally, in everything getting planted at the right time or, if I'm honest, somewhat close to the right time.

If I were planning on growing salad mix, broccoli, and watermelons, my calendar might look like this:

You'll notice that the game plan for salad mix looks a little different than the plan for broccoli and watermelons because it is planted at staggered intervals (succession planting). Gardeners often choose to plant multiple successions of salad mix to extend the length of time they can pick fresh greens. With careful planning, you can time your second planting to be harvest-ready just as your first planting, which you can generally harvest from a few times, starts winding down.

On this calendar, no salad mix is seeded during the heat of the summer. While it's not impossible to grow salad greens at this time, it is more difficult (and the lettuce just doesn't taste quite as good). Broccoli also prefers cooler conditions and is often planted in two successions, one that will mature early in the growing season and one that will mature toward the end.

Keep in mind that no matter how much we research and perfect our plan on paper, our timing will almost always be a little "off." Variances in weather, soil, and caretaking practices will influence plant health and how quickly the plants will reach maturity.

Depending on whether you're interested in starting your own seeds indoors or purchasing transplants, your calendar will look

PLANTING CALENDAR

APRIL

	1	2	3	4	5	6
7	8	9	10	11	12	13
14	15	16	17	18	19	20
		DS SALAD 1				
21	22	23	24	25	26	27
		START BROC 1 INDOORS				
28	29	30				
		DS SALAD 2				

MAY

		1	2	3	4
5	6 LAST FROST	8	9	10	11
	START W'MELON INDOORS				
12	13	14	15	16	17	18
		DS SALAD 3	H SALAD 1			
19	20	21	22	23	24	25
		T BROC 1				
26	27	28	29	30	31	
		DS SALAD 4	H SALAD 2			

JUNE

						1
2	3	4	5	6	7	8
		T W'MELON				
9	10	11	12	13	14	15
		H SALAD 3				
16	17	18	19	20	21	22
23 / 30	24	25	26	27	28	29
		H SALAD 4				

DS DIRECT SOW OUTDOORS

T TRANSPLANT OUTDOORS

H HARVEST

FROSTS ARE AVERAGES BASED ON LOCATION

JULY

	1	2	3	4	5	6
7	8	9	10	11	12	13
14	15	16	17	18	19	20
	START BROC 2 (FALL CROP)					
21	22	23	24	25	26	27
					H BROC 1	
28	29	30	31			

AUGUST

				1	2	3
4	5	6	7	8	9	10
11	12	13	14	15	16	17
		T BROC 2 (FALL CROP)			DS SALAD 5	
18	19	20	21	22	23	24
					H W'MELON	
25	26	27	28	29	30	31
	DS SALAD 6					

SEPTEMBER

1	2	3	4	5	6	7
8	9	10	11	12	13	14
	DS SALAD 7		H SALAD 5			
15	16	17	18	19	20	21
22	23	24	25	26	27	28
	DS SALAD 8		H SALAD 6			
29	30					

OCTOBER

		1	2	3	4	5
6	FIRST FROST	8	9	10	11	12
	H SALAD 7 (USE ROW COVER)					
13	14	15	16	17	18	19
				H BROC 2 (FALL CROP)		
20	21	22	23	24	25	26
	H SALAD 8 (USE ROW COVER)					
27	28	29	30	31		

a little different too. It's fun to start each season by growing things inside, but this requires space, adequate light, and extra time. If you decide to buy seedlings, ask local gardeners where to buy the healthiest plants; not all plant nurseries are created equal! (We'll discuss how to start seeds and purchase seedlings in chapter seven.)

How Much Should I Grow?

An easy way to approach the question of "how much" is to plan to grow more of your favorites and less of the rest, especially if you're growing something for the first time and you're not sure if you will like it! To start, you might decide, "I want to grow as much watermelon as possible, lots of salad mix, a bit of broccoli, and radishes wherever I can fit them."

You will, at some point in your life as a gardener, make the mistake of overplanting zucchini. Gardening writer Frank Tozer suggests one plant per person. In my opinion, a more reasonable ratio of zucchini plants to humans who eat zucchini is about 2:3; that's two plants for every three people who never get sick of it. Plant more than this and you will be making a job of giving it away (the romanticism of which sounds lovely at first but will likely wear off with time).

Where Should I Grow It?

Growing an assortment of vegetables, fruits, herbs, and flowers together will create a very different feel from growing clean, straight rows of single crops. Each approach has its appeal, and whichever you choose will obviously affect where you put what.

There are numerous other ways to decide the "where" of what will grow in your garden. You may want to organize sections of your garden by plant family, which will make crop rotation (changing where plant families grow each year) easier.

THE WET SLIPPER TEST

According to Bill Mollison, who formalized the idea of permaculture, if picking fresh herbs for your breakfast results in your slippers getting wet, then your herbs are too far away.

Fresh herbs just outside your door, perhaps in an herb spiral or container garden, encourage frequent gathering of herbs for your kitchen and spark culinary creativity.

Or you can organize them by when your plantings will be ready for harvest, or by what will create the most beautiful patterns of blooms, colors, and textures in your garden.

If you're short on time, planting your early-season crops together in one area and late-season crops in another allows you to focus your watering, weeding, and other caretaking efforts. If one of your goals is to create an interconnected garden ecosystem, you may wish to plant a variety of different plants in the same area which will encourage the development of ecological relationships (you'll learn more about companion planting on the next page). You may decide to grow your perennials in one place or have them integrated into your annual plantings.

Each year when I plan the "where" of a garden, I start off by organizing beds by plant families, then consider succession planting, companion planting, and interplanting. Plants that will be harvested from more frequently are assigned spots closer to the path, where they'll be easier to reach, and taller plants are allocated to the north side of a bed so they won't block sunlight from reaching shorter plants.

WAYS TO GARDEN LIKE NATURE

Interplanting and companion planting are just two of the many planting strategies people use to garden like nature. Consider whether either of these practices could work well as part of your garden plan.

Interplanting

Forests are excellent gardening teachers. In forests and other ecosystems, plants layer their growth in space and time. Forest mosses may have caught your eye in early spring, their vibrant green standing out in a mostly brown forest. Mosses take advantage of the extra sunlight reaching the forest floor before the forest canopy leafs out.

Interplanting is a technique that mimics this natural plant strategy, maximizes abundance by growing more food in the same amount of space, and leaves less bare ground susceptible to erosion, helping keep the soil biologically active.

For example, you may decide you also want to grow radishes, but your space is already reserved for watermelons, broccoli, and successions of salad mix. Since radishes grow quickly, need relatively little space, and can handle cool spring temperatures, you have some options for interplanting. You could seed the radishes in between your freshly transplanted broccoli seedlings; the radishes will mature and be ready to pick before the broccoli leaves shade them out. While not technically interplanting, you could also plant a couple successions of radishes in the early spring in the bed that's waiting for warmer temperatures and watermelon transplants.

Companion Planting

The Three Sisters plant guild (see page 89) is an example of companion planting, which simply means planting two or

FAMILY MATTERS

Learning which families your garden plants belong to can help you better understand the needs of your plants. Plants in the same family often need similar nutrients and environmental conditions and are susceptible to some of the same pests. Knowing plant families also helps gardeners with plant rotation (see Garden R&R on page 104).

Apiaceae: **carrots, celery, parsnip**

Brassicaceae: **bok choy, broccoli, brussels sprouts, cabbage, cauliflower, collard greens, kale, kohlrabi, radishes, and turnips**

Cucurbitaceae: **cucumbers, gourds, melons, pumpkins, summer and winter squash, zucchini**

Fabaceae (legumes): **beans and peas**

Liliaceae: **asparagus, garlic, leeks, onions, shallots**

Solanaceae (nightshades): **tomatoes, potatoes, eggplant, peppers, tomatillos**

Greens:* **arugula, lettuce, spinach, Swiss chard**

Annual herbs:* **basil, cilantro, dill, parsley**

Perennial herbs:* **chives, lemon balm, mint, oregano, rosemary, sage, savory, thyme**

*These plants, technically not in the same family, have been grouped together for the sake of simplicity.

more species of plants close together to benefit at least one of them. Sometimes one plant will deter pests from another, or one plant may have better flavor when the other is grown close by. Sometimes gardeners identify companion plants simply by making detailed observations over time, noting that at least one of the plants benefits without knowing the exact reason why. (You can find a list of plant companions on page 215.)

Every time I plan a garden, it is obvious how dependent these last three steps—when, how much, and where—are on each other. The planning process often looks more like a web of decisions than a linear progression. Attend to these final three steps in whichever order feels most relevant to your unique situation.

For gardeners working with limited growing space, considering "where" before "when" might make more sense. If you intend to grow the majority of the fresh produce that your family eats, you might think about "how much" first. "When" might be important to think about first if you have a very short growing season.

GARDEN R&R (REST & ROTATION)

Farmers and gardeners managing large growing spaces often plan to leave sections of their gardens fallow, allowing the soil to have a time of rest. A cover crop like buckwheat, winter rye grass, or a mix of oats and peas may be planted to keep the soil biologically active and protect it from erosion, but instead of harvesting the plants, the farmer or gardener turns the plant residue back into the ground (generally with the aid of a tiller, but you can make do with hand tools in a small garden), where it will decompose and enrich the soil. (More on this in chapter eight.)

JUST FOR LITTLE GARDENER
LETTING THE GARDEN TAKE A NAP

Did you know that garden beds need rest just like we do? After a few years of growing lots of food, the soil may need to take a nap. One way that you can help a garden bed rest is to tuck it in. Cover it with a two-inch blanket of compost and add two or three inches of straw. Let it sleep for the whole growing season. The following year, it will be rested and ready to grow!

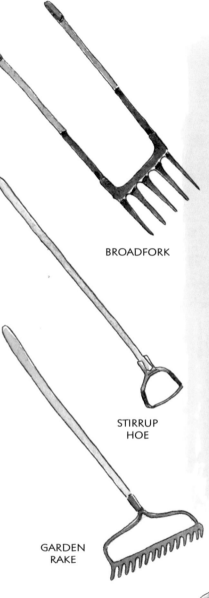

BROADFORK

STIRRUP
HOE

GARDEN
RAKE

WHAT TOOLS DO I NEED?

Gardeners tend to develop affinities for certain garden tools. Some simply *must* have a broadfork and stirrup hoe, while others have either never heard of them or don't find them useful. Since good tools can be expensive, try starting with just a few from "the basics" list. If you sense something's missing, take a gander under "nice but not necessary." All that said, I predict you will come to appreciate your hands as your most useful and dependable garden tool.

The Basics:

☐ Cultivator (what I like to call "the claw")
☐ Digging fork
☐ Garden rake
☐ Hand clippers
☐ Shovel
☐ Trowel

Nice but not necessary:

☐ Broadfork
☐ Collinear hoe
☐ Hoe (standard type)
☐ Spade (flat-edge)
☐ Stirrup or scuffle hoe

See page 217 for where to purchase tools just the right size for Little Gardener.

CULTIVATOR
a.k.a. "THE CLAW"

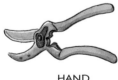

HAND
CLIPPERS

You may choose to let sections of your garden rest for a growing season. It's also important to rotate members of the same plant family so that you don't plant them in the same place every year. For example, after growing cauliflower in one area of your garden, ideally no other members of the Brassica family should be planted there for three years! Rotating your crops will help minimize pest and disease pressure in your garden.

SOURCING SEEDS

There are a variety of options for sourcing seeds:

- Check your local library to see if they have a community seed library or seed exchange.

- Buy seeds at a garden shop, plant nursery, grocery store, or hardware store.

- Order directly from a seed company's catalog or website (they usually offer the greatest variety of seeds).

- Small seed companies specializing in regionally adapted varieties seem to be sprouting up (pun intended) more and more; see if there are any in your area. Order seeds early— the popular varieties can go fast! (See page 218 for a list of seed companies that I've had great results with.)

ACTIVITIES

SOLVING THE GARDEN-PLAN PUZZLE

Bring the "what, when, how much, and where" pieces together in this activity to help summarize your garden plan.

You will need:

- ☐ Your garden map
- ☐ A list of what you want to grow and the information you've collected about each plant
- ☐ Your planting calendar
- ☐ Pencil
- ☐ Colored pencils
- ☐ Scissors
- ☐ Construction paper
- ☐ Glue
- ☐ Seed catalogs that you don't mind cutting up

Part I: Your Planting Calendar

Creating your own planting calendar will help you keep track of when to plant all of the things you and Little Gardener would like to grow:

1. On a blank calendar that you can devote exclusively to garden planning, note your average last frost date in the spring, and your average first frost date in the fall (see page 42). Do this in pencil (you'll see why in just a bit!).

2. For each vegetable, fruit, flower, or herb you plan to grow, note on your calendar when you should seed or transplant.

3. If you want to take it a step further, note when you can expect a harvest for each and how long it will last. Knowing

when the harvest period of one planting ends allows you to plan what to plant there next (which is especially helpful if you're short on space).

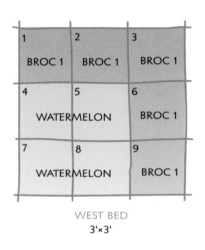

GARDEN MAP — SPRING

1	2	3
BROC 1	BROC 1	BROC 1
4	5	6
WATERMELON		BROC 1
7	8	9
WATERMELON		BROC 1

WEST BED
3'×3'

A	B
SALAD MIX 1	SALAD MIX 2
C	D
SALAD MIX 3	SALAD MIX 4

EAST BED
2'×2'

Part II: Your Garden Map

In this activity, you will create "puzzle pieces" representing what you'd like to grow. By moving the pieces around your garden map, you can plan your what, where, and how much:

1. Make a copy or two of your garden map, the one with the named beds and divided, labeled sections, and save your blank original.

2. Cut out pictures from old seed catalogs of what you want to grow.

PLANTING CALENDAR — SPRING

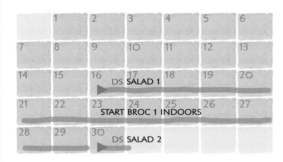

APRIL

	1	2	3	4	5	6
7	8	9	10	11	12	13
14	15	16 DS SALAD 1	17	18	19	20
21	22	23 START BROC 1 INDOORS	24	25	26	27
28	29	30 DS SALAD 2				

● EAST BED **A**

● EAST BED **A, B**

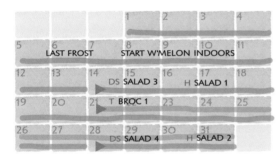

MAY

		1	2	3	4
5	6 LAST FROST	7	8 START W'MELON INDOORS	9	10	11
12	13	14 DS SALAD 3	15	16 H SALAD 1	17	18
19	20	21 T BROC 1	22	23	24	25
26	27	28 DS SALAD 4	29	30 H SALAD 2	31	

● EAST BED **A, B, C**

● WEST BED **1, 2, 3, 6, 9**

● EAST BED **ALL SECTIONS**

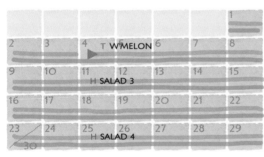

JUNE

						1
2	3	4 T W'MELON	5	6	7	8
9	10	11 H SALAD 3	12	13	14	15
16	17	18	19	20	21	22
23	24	25 H SALAD 4	26	27	28	29
30						

● WEST BED **ALL SECTIONS**

DS DIRECT SOW OUTDOORS
T TRANSPLANT OUTDOORS
H HARVEST
FROST IS AN AVERAGE BASED ON LOCATION

3. Glue your images on pieces of construction paper—bigger pieces for plants that will need more space, smaller ones for plants that will need less. For crops you want to grow more of, make more pieces. The size and number of pieces doesn't have to be perfect—only practical enough so that moving them around on your garden map is helpful for planning.

4. (For square-foot gardeners: Pre-make squares the size of a bed section on your map and note, on the back, the quantity of a specific crop that can be grown in 1 square foot. Glue pictures of your crop onto the squares.)

5. Make "puzzle" pieces for features that are part of your design—like secret nooks, tunnel trellises, and sunflower houses (see page 155).

6. To help remember which plants will thrive growing near each other, make "companion notes" on the backs of the papers or on a separate "cheat sheet."

7. Slide the plants and features around on your map between different beds and sections, experimenting with how things will fit together, like a puzzle.

8. Imagine walking through the garden you have just planned. How does what you see compare with how you've visualized your dream garden? How can you change your planting plan to more accurately reflect your dream?

Part III: Bringing the Pieces Together

Once you have a decent idea of when you'll be planting everything and where it will be planted, it's time to make sure that your "when" and "where" will work well together:

1. Make a copy or two of your planting calendar and save your original.

2. Assign a different colored pencil color to each of your beds and lightly shade over your writing on your planting calendar with the designated color to indicate which bed you will seed, transplant into, or harvest from. (See page 109.)

3. Within the shaded area, write the section number(s) or letter(s) to indicate specifically where in the bed a particular plant will be planted.

Does the puzzle fit together?

Check your calendar for any gaps—times when, or spaces where, nothing is planted. Circle back to your "how much" notes and make any adjustments to the puzzle. If there are some open spots, review your plant list to see if you can find something that would be a good fit for that space.

CHANGING THE "WHEN TO GROW IT"

What can you create in your garden to help you start growing earlier or keep growing later? Microclimates! A simple structure like a cold frame can help you extend your growing season.

A cold frame is a "growing box" with a clear top that allows sunlight in and traps heat, like a mini-greenhouse. Arrange a few straw bales for the frame and place old windows on top,

or make a true box fashioned from wood with an old framed window for a hinged lid. It is the perfect size minigarden for a Little Gardener and would be a fun project for the two of you to do together!

JOURNAL PROMPTS

- If a forest had a "gardener," what might their garden plan look like?
- If a pond had a "gardener," what might their garden plan look like?
- What was your favorite part of solving the garden-plan puzzle?
- What was the most challenging part of solving the garden-plan puzzle?

CHAPTER REVIEW

- Planning a garden involves four essential steps: deciding *what* to grow, *when* to grow it, *how much* to grow, and *where* to grow it.

- Before you plan your garden, get to know the needs and quirks of your plants.

- "Garden like nature" by planning diverse garden beds and using techniques like companion planting and interplanting.

IN THE NEXT CHAPTER...

You have likely encountered some variation of Allen Saunders's quote "Life is what happens to us while we are making other plans." Plans are handy to have but you and your garden will grow in ways you can't possibly plan. Embrace the wondrous uncertainty that lies ahead and be ready to adjust your plans if needed. Your garden design and plan will come to life as you physically build the structures and soil that will grow the dream. It's time to gather your tools and get outside.

CHAPTER SIX
CREATING

Build structures and soil

In *The New Organic Grower*, author Eliot Coleman—considered by some to be the modern-day grandfather of organic growing—writes, "The determined farmer can transform even the most unlikely site into a model farm by applying the basic techniques of soil building." One of my first garden interns at Tomten Farm and dearest friends, Taya Schulte, operates Growing Lots Urban Farm in Minneapolis, Minnesota, with partner Seamus Fitzgerald. Their farm sits on top of a parking lot.

Soil is the foundation of any farm or garden. Using a mixture of wood chips, leaves, organic food scraps, beer mash, kitchen compost, and coffee chaff (all from neighbors and local businesses), Taya and Seamus, the farmers who cared for the space before them, and billions of soil organisms worked to build the twelve inches of soil that would become the living foundation of the farm.

Growing Lots provides vegetables to seventy neighborhood families throughout the growing season through their CSA (community supported agriculture) member program. An integral part of the neighborhood, Growing Lots, just like everything in nature, is part of a web of resources and is woven into the fabric of the community, both the human systems and the more ecological ones. The farm functions as a food source, a recycler of natural materials, and a place for community

PRAYERS ON A PARKING LOT

Some years before Taya and Seamus took over the business, Growing Lots came into being with a whole lot of community support, funding, and compost. Before the hard work of building soil began, an unusual thing happened as part of the creation process: community members wrote blessings and prayers for the farm-to-be on the surface of the parking lot. A pond liner was laid over the farm blessings, protecting the soil-to-be from any potential toxins. Seamus and Taya work closely with the University of Minnesota's Department of Soil, Water, and Climate, who study their soil and regularly test for harmful contaminants.

gatherings, and offers educational opportunities that connect people with the land and soil that feeds them.

PREPARING SPACES FOR YOUR GARDEN BEDS

Physically building the beds and fundamental structures you've been dreaming about, designing on paper, and literally sketching out on the land with stakes and twine, is a satisfying experience.

You can create a garden at any time of year, but autumn is best. If you build your beds and prepare the soil before winter sets in, you'll be ahead of the game come spring—especially if very wet springs and heavy soils are a part of your reality.

Before you break fresh ground or start building on top of existing ground, revisit your garden design. Review the shape and layout of the garden as a whole, and then confirm the placement of special design features.

To Break Ground or Not to Break Ground

Giving structure to your dream garden may involve breaking ground, or it may not. Assuming you are starting with a mowed lawn and plan on using a combination of human power and hand tools, here are a few garden bed creation options to consider. Describe the possibilities to Little Gardener and discuss which feels like the best fit for your land, mission, and guiding principles.

Don't Dig, Just Build

Leave the grass in place and smother it by building a raised bed on top of it.

To smother the grass and keep it from growing up into your bed, lay down thick overlapping layers of newspaper or cardboard. Cover a slightly larger footprint than you've planned for your beds, which will give them some breathing room. Although this approach is minimally disruptive to the existing soil, you do lose the benefits of integrating existing soil life and organic matter into your garden. With this option, you'll be importing topsoil—which is relatively inexpensive—or creating it yourself (see composting and lasagna gardening later in this chapter).

Break Ground, Build a Raised Bed

Dig up the grass, remove it, and then build a raised bed on top of it.

Alternatively, you can dig up the sod, flip it over (so the grass is face down and the roots and soil are face up), and chop it up with a shovel to break up any large clumps; this keeps precious organic matter in place to decompose. Remaining clumps can be broken up with additional spading sessions over a period of several weeks.

Many gardeners swear by the "trick" of flipping sod upside down. I have had a difficult time trusting this approach. The roots of some grasses are voraciously aggressive, and I haven't yet been convinced that flipping them upside down compromises their willpower.

Completely digging up your grass lets you start with your garden footprint mostly free of plant matter. Removing the sod subtracts some of the microorganisms and organic matter in the top layer of soil, but this can be mitigated by shaking as much soil out of the roots as possible. You'll likely have fewer weeds and you'll start off with less clumpy soil.

Break Ground, Grow Directly in It
Dig up the grass, flip it over or remove it, and then create a ground-level bed.

For ground-level beds, break ground and manage grass as described above. Add some topsoil and compost to the cleared area to bring it back up to ground level, since removing the grass and roots removes some soil too. Work in the new material with a garden rake, hoe, or other cultivating tool. Alternatively, you might want to build your own soil right on site.

With any of the above approaches, be sure to cover the bed to protect it from erosion until you are ready to plant. You can use a mulch such as straw, grass clippings, leaves, cardboard, or thick layers of newspaper, which will also enrich the soil.

Note: Many gardeners have no issue with tossing the discarded clumps of grass and roots into their regular compost pile. Again, I'm suspicious of the grass's overly ambitious tendencies and prefer to let them decompose in a pile separate from the one I plan to use on my vegetable garden.

DON'T BE AFRAID TO EXPERIMENT

When Taya and I worked together at Tomten Farm, we, along with many helpers, built curved raised beds with keyhole paths in the geodesic grow dome. The beds were made from rebar, chicken wire, and cement. After driving rebar into the soil every one or two feet, we folded a couple layers of chicken wire over it and then "mushed" cement into the wire "frame," completely covering it, and then smoothed out the cement surface. This was an experiment, since we lacked technical expertise, and during our time on the mesa it served as a beautiful and effective growing space.

BUILDING RAISED BEDS

In chapter four, I introduced the many benefits of raised beds, including their improved drainage, ability to warm up faster than surrounding soil, and tendency to remain less compacted.

Borderless Beds

You may choose to create raised beds with or without borders. Borderless raised beds do not have a hard perimeter structure that keeps soil in place. Instead, soil is raked up to form a flat-topped "mesa" that is higher than the ground surrounding it. As the soil settles throughout the season, some upkeep is required to maintain the bed's volume and shape—you may need to add material and rake soil in from the edges. It does, however, offer the freedom to change the bed's shape with relative ease. Going borderless is especially practical if you don't have access to border materials, if the cost of such materials doesn't fit your budget, or if you're planning on creating large or creatively shaped beds.

Beds with Borders

Raised beds with borders are pleasing to the eye. With borders, you can make your beds as deep as you like, creating a comfortable height for differently abled and differently sized gardeners.

Little Gardener may enjoy fashioning borders from stones, logs, or stumps, or old cinder blocks—let them see what they can find in the yard! Get creative with what you have lying around, but be sure to choose materials that are free of toxins (no painted or pressure-treated wood, old railroad ties, etc.).

While raised beds made from lumber are more of an investment, they are quite attractive. Building your own raised bed box is an easy way to include Little Gardener in the garden creation process (see page 131). Let Little Gardener do as much of the work as possible.

CREATING YOUR PATHS

When you walked through your imaginary garden in chapter one, what did the path feel like under your feet? Soft grass, loose gravel, wood chips?

If you've created your beds amidst a lawn, the path of least resistance is obviously grass. Presumably, you already have the equipment—a lawnmower and/or a Weedwacker—to attend to mowing and edging. For ground-level beds, you will undoubtedly need to combat the spread of grass from the paths into the beds, unless you invest in barriers you can sink into the soil.

Remember, though, grass is not afraid to push boundaries and will eventually find a way around them. Raised beds are more effective at preventing grass from weaseling its way in at the edges.

Bits of dirt and seeds will eventually float in on the wind and deposit themselves on paths of any kind. After a time, though perhaps invisible to your eyes, enough small pockets of organic matter will form to host seed growth above the weed fabric. Nature will find a way. It always does.

Living Paths

Some gardeners dig up their grass and sow a low-growing perennial clover as an alternative ground cover and for a different look. If you go this route, allow plenty of time for the clover to fully establish itself before it has to contend with heavy foot traffic. If it gets too tall for your liking, mow it and rake the trimmings onto your beds as a nutrient-rich top-dressing for the soil. Just make sure the clover hasn't started to produce any seeds yet, since then you'd effectively be planting weeds into your garden.

While the clover, like grass, will also eventually make its way into borderless or ground-level beds, you may find comfort in knowing that some gardeners intentionally plant clover under their vegetable crops to fix nitrogen and protect the soil from erosion. (More about living mulch in chapter eight.)

Note: Clover attracts bees when it is flowering, which is wonderful for your garden and the bees, but I'd advise against planting it as an extensive ground cover if you are allergic to beestings.

Gravel Paths

Inviting and pleasing to the eye, gravel paths also offer the promise of less maintenance. Usually, gravel is spread on top of a weed barrier or landscape fabric after grass and roots have been removed. Weed fabric does help keep weeds at bay, but depending on how aspirational your weeds are, it will not hold them back indefinitely.

Wood Chip Paths

Wood chips give paths a natural feel and can be placed right on bare soil or over weed fabric. Unlike gravel, wood chips will eventually break down (adding nutrients to the soil) and will need to be replenished every few years. Some tree service companies will drop off wood chips at no charge if they complete a job nearby, making them an attractive choice for the economical gardener.

FENCES

If you feel a fence is necessary, the kind you choose will depend on what your goals are, the surface you're working with, and, of course, what you are trying to keep out.

Metal or wooden posts can be pounded into the ground with a post pounder, mallet, or sledge hammer. Plastic mesh or metal-wire fencing can be wrapped around the posts and attached with wire twists or zip ties. In *The New Organic Grower*, Eliot Coleman discusses his fondness for different types of plastic mesh fencing, which he has found to be very effective in keeping out a variety of animals ranging from raccoons to deer.

You may have come across "living fences," or "natural fences," plantings of dense vegetation that create a boundary to deter or prevent larger creatures or humans from passing through it. While I've never grown one myself, I'd like to—especially on a site where it could double as a windbreak—and see how well it keeps out unwanted guests.

If you are working with raised beds on a constructed surface like a parking lot, or if you have shallow topsoil, screw your wooden fence posts directly to your raised bed. A simple entrance can be fashioned by not permanently attaching the last few feet of fencing, so you can fold it back at the last point of attachment, like a door on a hinge.

If your garden consists of one raised bed, you will need to create a small path on the bed itself. Create a small keyhole-shaped path (see page 91) by placing a wide board or stepping stones on the soil to designate where to step. If you have multiple raised beds, you can wrap the entire area with mesh fencing and line up your entrance with an existing path.

If you have an urgent and dire need to defend the garden, electric fencing is an option, either as a moveable electric fence (types for poultry and sheep are relatively affordable) or as an added electric wire strung above your other fencing and out of reach of Little Gardeners. My dad, an avid gardener, knows all too well that there is nothing like raccoons eating the bulk of your sweet corn overnight to motivate you to install electric fencing the very next day.

SOIL: THE LIVING FOUNDATION OF THE GARDEN

When I got my first good look at the soil in the Learning Garden, and felt it with my hands, I was certain I could use it to make bricks, build a shelter, and fashion my own plates and cups. Heavy clay soils were what I was used to, so this was not my first rodeo, but I had a lot of work ahead of me.

Life on Earth is as dependent on soil as it is on air, water, and sunlight; soil is the foundation upon which terrestrial ecosystems grow. Healthy soil is a prerequisite for a healthy, abundant garden. Building and taking care of soil is the single most proactive thing a gardener can do to promote their garden's success.

Soil Basics

Soil sediments of sand, silt, and clay are formed as rocks break down into smaller and smaller pieces over long periods of time. Loam, a mixture of these sediments and organic matter, has the loose, crumbly soil texture that is ideal for a garden.

Sediment gives structure to the soil ecosystem, which is made up of air, water, insects, worms, microbes, nutrients from decomposed organic matter (like leaves, twigs, and animal waste), and small animals (like rodents and snakes) that use it as habitat. One teaspoon of soil could contain one billion bacteria and tens and even hundreds of thousands of fungi and algae! The more soil life your garden has, the healthier and more resilient your garden will be.

Microbes, insects, fungi, and earthworms help decompose organic material, such as plant and animal wastes, into nutrients that plants can take up. Holes made by worms and other animals keep the soil loose so that roots can easily grow and water can percolate through the soil to reach those roots.

RECOMMENDED READING FOR LITTLE GARDENER

In Steve Tomecek's book *Dirt*, part of National Geographic's Jump into Science series, Little Gardener can follow an adventurous star-nosed mole underground to learn more about soil, how it's formed, and how important it is to life on Earth.

DIRT

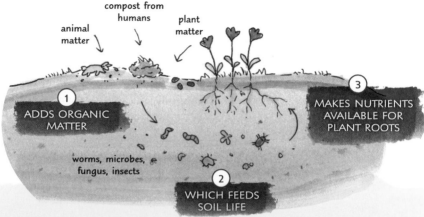

compost from humans

animal matter

plant matter

1 ADDS ORGANIC MATTER

3 MAKES NUTRIENTS AVAILABLE FOR PLANT ROOTS

worms, microbes, fungus, insects

2 WHICH FEEDS SOIL LIFE

JUST FOR LITTLE GARDENER
SOIL BASICS

Healthy gardens need healthy soil. Soil is an ecosystem made of up of living things, like earthworms and microbes (tiny creatures we can't see), and non-living things, like sediment and air. The living things in the soil turn dead stuff and waste into nutrients that plants can use to grow. Soil also provides plants with minerals and water.

Soil feeds the plants we eat, the trees we use for building, the cotton plants we make clothes from, and the grasses dairy cows eat so they can produce milk. We also create landscapes by moving soil around. Without soil, life would be hard for people and many living things!

TAKING CARE OF SOIL

Soil erosion is an environmental issue that many people aren't aware of. We are losing soil faster than nature can replenish it. Depending on the climate in a given area, it can take hundreds or thousands of years to form one inch of soil.

As gardeners, we can take good care of our soil by doing the following:

- covering bare soil with garden plantings or mulch to help prevent soil erosion

- adding organic matter to our soil, which feeds soil life

- walking on paths to prevent the garden soil from becoming compacted (diminishing room for water, air, roots, and soil life)

- growing plants in a natural way, without using pesticides or herbicides that kill soil life

Organic Matter & pH

If you pay attention to only two characteristics of your soil as you're creating your garden, let those two things be pH and organic matter.

Any soil type generally improves in quality with the addition of organic matter. This is the method—along with heavily mulching our beds each autumn—that we used to turn the hard and heavy clay soil of the Learning Garden into soil that you could easily sink your hand into wrist-deep. If your garden soil consists of at least 5 percent organic matter, you're in good shape; closer to 10 percent is amazing. Keeping your soil rich with organic matter ensures your soil microbes are happy, and keeping your soil microbes happy keeps your plants happy, and happy plants make for happy gardeners.

In addition to plenty of organic matter, plants need soil that has a balanced acidity, or pH. You can test the pH of your soil with a simple soil test from your local home and garden center (or through a professional soil testing service, which will measure pH, organic matter, and much more).

Most garden vegetables require a soil pH of between 6.0 and 7.0—slightly acidic—and will not thrive in soil outside of their preferred range. Certain plants like blueberries prefer very acidic soil (4.5–5.0). The pH scale is logarithmic, with values ranging from 1 to 14, 1 being the most acidic, 7 being neutral, and 14 being the most alkaline.

There are ways to amend your soil to adjust the pH if necessary. Adding organic matter and compost is the best way to lower your pH (making soil more acidic), while adding limestone or wood ash raises it (making soil more alkaline). You can reach out to your local agricultural extension office for assistance with soil testing or modifying your soil.

BUILDING YOUR OWN SOIL

The phrase "building soil" may sound a little strange to new gardeners, but it is one of the most fun and interesting ways to cocreate with nature!

Composting

"What does composting mean?" I asked the group of third-graders.

"It means throwing your leftovers into the woods."

"Not quite, but you're onto something," I smiled. "Does anyone have a compost pile at home?" A few hands went up. "What is it for?"

"It's for recycling food. Worms and bugs eat the food and their poop makes plant food."

RECOMMENDED READING FOR BIG GARDENER

Gardening expert Dick Raymond, author of Garden Way's *Joy of Gardening*—and host of an old television series by the same name—provides instructions on how to modify your soil pH, create garden beds, and prepare soil, and offers many other golden nuggets of information in his book. While it's clear he has a greater affinity than I for mechanical tillers, I find his general advice to be spot-on, easy to apply, and timeless.

"Yes! That's exactly right. When we create a compost pile, the material we put in there will decompose, which means it will break down into smaller and smaller pieces with the help of worms, insects, bacteria, and fungus. Eventually it will become nutrient-rich soil, and you can mix it into your garden soil for your plants to use as food."

The rules for composting are simple:

Do . . .

- [ ] keep the pile moist and aerated, which will help manage temperature and encourage decomposition

- [ ] balance carbon-rich material (dry "browns," such as leaves, newspaper, straw, wood shavings, peat moss) with nitrogen-rich material (wetter "greens," grass clippings, kitchen scraps, leftovers from your plate)

- [ ] add animal bedding, such as straw, pine shavings, sawdust (see "browns" above)

- [ ] add manure (considered to be a "green" since it is nitrogen-rich) from animals like rabbits, horses, goats, sheep, and alpacas

Don't . . .

- [ ] add any dairy, meat, or oily or heavily processed foods (these can take longer to break down and attract uninvited mammalian guests)

- [ ] add any sick or diseased plant matter

- [ ] add manure from cats or dogs (or people!)

A compost pile should be at least one cubic yard to be of good use to you and your garden. This size allows the temperature in the center of the pile to get hot enough to kill diseases and weed seeds. (I've heard rumors of a farmer who slow-roasted a small turkey in his compost pile!) You can check to see if your pile is "cooking" by taking its temperature with a compost thermometer—the ideal range is 113–158 °F (45–70 °C). Some gardeners use the heat from compost piles to warm their greenhouses!

A healthy, well-balanced compost pile should smell good and earthy; a stinky pile usually means there's too much moisture and not enough air, or that nitrogen-rich materials are overabundant. In this case, mix more "browns" into the pile. You can always ask your neighbors for fallen leaves from their yards (just be sure they don't spray any chemicals on their lawns).

If your pile is not heating up, it may need more moisture or oxygen, or your soil microbes might be hungry! Try mixing in more "greens," adding some water if the pile appears very dry, and then turning the pile to aerate it. Be patient; compost piles may take some time to get going.

Mix your pile twice a week, or whenever you think to do so, to incorporate new matter and air—the pile will be more productive the more you turn it. Compost is ready when it looks like rich, crumbly soil and has no remaining identifiable chunks of organic material (with the exception of the tiniest eggshell pieces).

Allowing Little Gardener to chop kitchen scraps into smaller pieces and deliver them to the compost pile is an easy way for them to help take care of the soil and feel part of the garden's cycles.

Don't have space for a compost pile? You can still compost your kitchen scraps using vermiculture (worm composting). See page 217 for resources.

Lasagna Gardening

Every fall in the forests near where I live, the trees lose their leaves, which form a carpet of nutrients-to-be on the forest floor. As the leaves decompose, the soil is enriched.

A method called *lasagna gardening* mimics that same process. By layering leaves and other organic materials and allowing them to compost "in place" over time, you feed the soil food web and help generate nutrient-rich soil for your plants. If the "no-till, no dig" approach appeals to you, this method is for you. Lasagna gardening is the easiest way for a Little Gardener to create a garden bed and build nutrient-rich soil at the same time.

You can build a lasagna garden at any time of year but doing it in autumn, when fallen leaves are plentiful, will make it even easier. Feel free to let your lasagna garden "cook" over the winter, or transplant seedlings into it right after you've built it.

If you are direct-seeding, first top your lasagna with finely textured compost or damp peat moss, and then tuck your seeds into that top layer. Roots will begin to travel downward and find places that will make them very happy.

MAKING THE GARDEN A SPECIAL PLACE FOR LITTLE GARDENER

Taking extra time to create features just for Little Gardener will offer more opportunities for them to connect with the garden. Harness the affection children have for building and playing in forts by including Little Gardener in the construction of special garden structures.

Trellises: Places for Plants to Climb
A trellis is anything that a plant climbs or uses for support and some plants must have a trellis in order to grow properly. You can build a simple trellis by getting creative with materials that you

HELPFUL HINT
CREATE A GARDEN SUPPLY BOX FOR LITTLE GARDENER

Include: safety scissors, seeds, a trowel, a ruler, laminated garden map and dry erase marker, popsicle sticks (and a permanent, fade-resistant marker—if you wish) for labeling plantings, and garden gloves.

may have lying around. For example, you can tie off lengths of twine between two or more posts you've set in the ground, creating a string "wall" for plants to climb, or create a tepee trellis (see activity at the end of this chapter).

My friend Karen Martin at Back to the Farm in Kinderhook, New York, grows gourds and other climbing plants on a huge tunnel trellis. It's made from "hooped" panels of metal fencing— even an adult can walk through or relax in it.

Signs Are Special Too

Don't underestimate the power and joy of good signage. Simple signs like "Baird Family Garden" or "Nate's Secret Garden Spot" reinforce your relationship with the garden and encourage stewardship of the space. Signs with the names and pictures of what's growing will help Little Gardener (and perhaps Big Gardener too) remember where everything is planted, learn to identify plants, and be better able to see and interpret interactions between members of the garden ecosystem. And, of course, painting signs will be a fun project for Little Gardener!

Boosting Your Garden's Wow Factor

Incorporating unexpected human objects into your garden space can create a striking contrast between human systems and natural ones. By repurposing an old wooden ladder as a trellis, a retired rubber boot as a planting container, or a bathtub as a place to play, you can turn a run-of-the-mill vegetable garden into a magical place for Little Gardeners.

ACTIVITIES

Building garden structures together is a wonderful way for you and Little Gardener to connect with each other and the garden.

BUILD A SIMPLE RAISED BED

This easy-to-build bed frame is nine square feet. It's adapted from the book *Square Foot Gardening with Kids* by Mel Bartholemew.

You will need:

- Four (4) wooden 2" × 6" boards (cedar, black locust, or fir are best), 3 feet long
- Pencil and ruler
- Power drill
- Drill bits and screw bits
- Twelve (12) 3-inch deck screws

1. Organize your tools and materials on a clear, flat surface.

2. Label each board with a letter: A, B, C, and D.

3. On each end of boards A and B, use board C as a guide and mark its width with your pencil (this is where the boards will overlap).

4. Between the end of the board and the mark, predrill three evenly spaced holes across the height of the board. Use a drill bit that is approximately

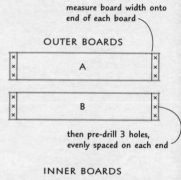

measure board width onto end of each board

OUTER BOARDS

A

B

then pre-drill 3 holes, evenly spaced on each end

INNER BOARDS

C

D

all boards equal in length

the width of the shaft of the screw. Predrilling holes helps prevent the board from cracking when you set your screws in. Elevate the board so you don't accidentally drill into your surface.

5. Carefully screw boards together as shown.

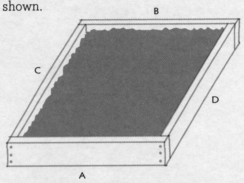

Other options and notes:

For extra sturdiness, you may choose to use L-brackets to secure the corners, or to add blocks of wood to the inside corners (the boards can be screwed into this block).

If you plan to place your raised bed on a deck or patio, make a bottom for it with a sheet of plywood (preferably a nontoxic type) and lay a tarp or other liner beneath the bed to protect the surface of the deck. Having a bottom on a small raised bed might even allow you to bring your garden with you if you move to a new place.

Local garden supply stores carry a variety of prefab raised beds and kits, and the National Gardening Association has instructional videos online for building garden beds, and for many other gardening projects too.

A QUICK LASAGNA GARDEN ON A LAWN

Here's a simple way to start a lasagna garden, adapted from *Lasagna Gardening* by Patricia Lanza. You can choose to add borders or build your lasagna within a raised bed.

You will need:

- ☐ Wooden stakes
- ☐ Twine
- ☐ Scissors
- ☐ Cardboard or newspaper (enough to thickly cover ground)

- ☐ "Brown" and "green" matter (see page 127)
- ☐ Compost
- ☐ Potting soil

1. Stake out the perimeter of your garden bed.

2. Lay down overlapping pieces of cardboard or thick layers of newspaper on top of mowed grass.

3. Layer "browns" and "greens" (and a few ½-inch to 1-inch layers of compost) until you have 18–24 inches of material stacked up. The volume ratio of browns to greens should be about 4:1.

4. A couple inches of finished compost (or mix of potting soil and compost) near the top will create a more favorable environment for seedlings.

BUILD A TEPEE TRELLIS

Tepee trellises are my favorite kind of trellises to create and are an eye-catching garden feature. Plants can climb the trellis *and* it can serve as a special place for Little Gardeners.

You will need:

- ☐ Three (3) or more 6- to 7-foot-tall wooden stakes (avoid smooth ones which will allow the twine to slip)
- ☐ Twine
- ☐ Scissors
- ☐ Step stool
- ☐ Sledge hammer (if necessary, to help set posts)

1. Push three or more wooden stakes into the soil so they lean toward each other in a triangle or circle formation, and tie them together near the top.

2. Walk around the tepee (avoid compacting the soil) and wrap twine around each stake, creating a "wall" of twine "levels," each 3–4 inches apart. This will allow climbing vines to form walls around the tepee. Be sure to leave one section "untwined" to serve as an entrance for Little Gardener.

3. Ensure that the lowest level of twine is no more than 3–4 inches above the soil so that the plants can easily find it.

4. Pole beans (natural climbers) and nasturtium (which can be trained to climb) are great candidates for being planted under a tepee trellis. Come summer, Little Gardener will be able to pick and snack on fresh beans and nasturtium flowers and leaves from the comfortable shade of their secret spot.

CONTAINER GARDEN BASICS

Not having a yard doesn't mean you can't create a garden. You can have a large or small garden on your deck, balcony, windowsill, or in any other sunny spot (at least six hours per day) by growing plants in a variety of containers.

Even if you do have a yard, it's convenient to keep frequently used plants, such as herbs, a little closer to your house. Remember Bill Mollison's Wet Slipper Test? (See page 101.)

You will need:

- ☐ Planting containers (planting pots, buckets, milk jugs, livestock trough)
- ☐ Tray to place containers on, if desired
- ☐ Power drill and drill bits
- ☐ Potting soil and compost
- ☐ Seeds or seedlings
- ☐ Mulch for the soil surface
- ☐ Popsicle sticks and UV-resistant marker

1. Review your list of what you would like to grow and how much space each plant needs.

2. Choose a container size that will allow your plant(s) to thrive.

3. Clean the container, and drill holes in the bottom for drainage. Put the container on a tray without holes if you need to protect the surface below.

4. Fill the container with a mix of potting soil and compost.

5. Transplant seedlings, or seed directly, into the container, and make a label for what you've planted there.

Note: Container gardens dry out faster than in-ground plantings, so be sure to water them regularly. Adding compost and a little mulch on top will help your soil retain moisture.

JOURNAL PROMPTS

- Who or what besides you is acting as a creator in your garden?
- What items in your house could still be produced if soil no longer existed?
- How can you tie your garden into your human and ecological neighborhoods? (See Growing Lots story on page 114.)

CHAPTER REVIEW

- The first step in creating your garden is preparing space for the beds in which you will plant your crops.

- Garden paths are important and there are many options for materials—grass, wood chips, gravel, or a living mulch-like clover.

- Building and taking care of soil is the single most proactive thing a gardener can do to promote their garden's success.

- Unusual features and structures can make the garden an extra special place for Little Gardeners.

IN THE NEXT CHAPTER...

A garden ecosystem thrives in soil that is rich in organic matter and abundant with soil life. Successfully cocreating with nature to build soil, mindfully crafting the structure of your garden based on your intentions, and including exciting features for Little Gardener will lay the foundation for growing a garden that will invite you both in. Now it's time to bring it to life.

GROWING YOUR GARDEN

CHAPTER SEVEN
PLANTING

Bring the garden to life

One tiny seed rested in the palm of my hand as I walked around to show the small group of students, parents, and teachers. "This seed will grow to be a head of lettuce," I said. They leaned in to take a closer look. Among the "ooos" and "whoas," one of the moms raised her eyebrows, looked up at me in amazement, and said, "This one little seed grows a whole head of lettuce?" I smiled and nodded. "That's fly," she said.

Cultivating a plant from seed through to maturity—so that it can become food that nourishes us—engages a deep and instinctual part of our being. It reminds us that our actions matter, that they have real results. Children visiting the Learning Garden had the opportunity to participate in every aspect of growing food, from planting seeds to preparing and enjoying a meal together.

BRINGING IT ALL TO LIFE, STARTING WITH SEEDS

Nature is impressive, and seeds—they are pure magic. If there's soil to grow in and the right amount of water and warmth, they know what to do. Inside them are the blueprints they need in order to grow into the plants that feed us and other animals.

Seeds are covered in a coat that protects them until they are met with just the right conditions to break their dormancy and germinate. Inside the coat are the beginnings of the root and stem of the plant, along with a small reserve of food to get the seed started on its journey of growth. Denise Pizzini, a flower farmer and garden educator friend of mine likes to say, "Seeds carry their own lunch!"

In nature, plants use different seed dispersal strategies for finding suitable spots to grow. Wind or water may transport seeds. Animals may transport seeds, such as burrs that stick to their fur, or carry seeds inside of them from the fruit that they ate! Some seeds need to go through an animal's digestive system before they germinate, while other seeds need to be exposed

RECOMMENDED READING FOR LITTLE GARDENER

A Seed Is Sleepy, a children's book by Dianna Hutts Aston, beautifully illustrates and tells stories about how different seeds sleep, wake up, travel, and grow. Ruth Krauss's *The Carrot Seed* is a board book classic for the Littlest Gardeners about a boy and his faith that a seed will grow.

to fire. Squirrels intentionally move acorns and other seeds, and bury them to store them as food for winter; inevitably, they forget about some of them, which may end up sprouting into oak trees in the spring.

Of course, in the garden, it is you who sows the seeds. Properly stored, most garden vegetable seeds are viable for two to five years, except for anything in the onion family, which only lasts about a year. When I inventory my seed collection each winter, I inevitably come across seeds that are past their "best-by" date. I mix them all up and scatter them in an empty spot in the garden and label it "mystery plot." Sometimes I'll massage the seeds into the soil, pat the soil down, and water them. Other times, I just let them be—I like seeing what nature is capable of doing without me.

LIFE OF A PLANT: HOW A PLANT GROWS

All garden seeds like to be planted in loose, fine-textured, rich, crumbly soil and to have the soil "tucked in" around them. Every plant's seeds have specific conditions that must be met for the

SEEDS THAT SLEPT FOR THOUSANDS OF YEARS

Occasionally, researchers and archaeologists find seeds that humans stored a long time ago, and modern-day plant scientists attempt to germinate them. Two-thousand-year-old date palm seeds found in Masada, Israel, were successfully germinated in 2005, and as of 2015, the sapling—which they named Methuselah—was still thriving.

Plant tissue from 32,000-year-old seeds, found encased in ice under 124 feet of permafrost, was used to regenerate an ancient variety of *Silene stenophylla*, an herbaceous, flowering plant native to Siberia.

SEEDS ARE ASLEEP

Most plants start their lives as seeds and most seeds need five things to sprout: soil, water, air, warmth, and space. (Sound familiar? Everything that seeds need in order to live, humans also need in order to live. Plants are part of nature, and so are we!)

Even before they are planted, seeds are alive, though they don't look like it. They're just sleeping! Seeds are covered in a seed coat that protects them until conditions are just right. Most vegetable seeds like to be tucked into dark soil, without light. They have a built-in alarm clock that tells them when to germinate. Germinate means to wake up, break open, and send a root down into the soil and a green shoot up toward the sun. Most garden vegetable seeds stay alive for a few years, but after that, they may not sprout.

germination process to kick in—they need to be planted at a certain depth and when the soil is in their preferred temperature range. Most garden vegetable seeds will do just fine if you plant them as they are, but some flower and tree seeds need special treatment, like exposure to cold temperatures (cold stratification) or help breaking open their seed coat (seed scarification). Pea and bean seeds benefit from being wrapped in a wet cloth and resting overnight before planting.

What Happens When a Seed Wakes Up?
Germination is the process of a seed waking up, splitting open, and sprouting. After planting, the seed starts absorbing water from the soil, and the seed coat begins to crack. The first root ventures down into the soil to gather water. The root also anchors the plant as the first shoot grows upward and breaks through the soil surface. The root "knows" to grow downward and the shoot "knows" to grow upward because the seed can sense gravity—this is known as *geotropism*.

DESCRIBING SEEDLING STAGES TO LITTLE GARDENER

For the Littlest Gardeners, I find it helpful to describe the different growth stages of seedlings (those that are started indoors and later transplanted outside), as grade levels in school. Seedlings that have recently sprouted, are tender and delicate, and still need the protection of the greenhouse are "preschoolers."

When they have matured a bit, usually after a few weeks, seedlings graduate to "kindergarten" and are ready to be hardened off. This means it's time for them to be moved from the comfortable growing conditions of the greenhouse to a semiprotected spot outside, where they can start becoming more comfortable being outside.

Through this process, kindergarten seedlings become hardy and better prepared for the harsher conditions they will experience in the garden. Once they are big and strong enough to be transplanted from their pot into the garden, seedlings are ready to advance to first grade!

Seedlings use the food stored in their seeds until their first true leaves form and they can begin to create their own food through the process of photosynthesis. With light from the sun (absorbed by the pigment chlorophyll), carbon dioxide, and water, plants make glucose (energy in the form of sugar) and also release oxygen as a waste product. Plants combine the energy they get from the sun with the nutrients and minerals they gather from the soil to nourish themselves and develop into mature plants.

Flowers: Formation, Pollination, Seed Production

Like animals, plants are driven to reproduce. Most plants do so by manufacturing their own seeds. As part of this process, and only when the time is right, a plant begins to form flowers.

Some plants, like cucumbers and melons, have separate male and female flowers. Others, like tomatoes and peppers, have male and female parts within the same single flower. Nectar in the flowers attracts pollinators like birds, bees, butterflies, and other insects, who move pollen within and between flowers. Corn and many grain crops use the wind to move pollen between plants. Pollen fertilizes an egg within the ovary of the female flower, enabling seeds to develop (right where the flower was blooming). Some plants enclose their seeds in fruit—I'm sure you've noticed the seeds inside

COMMON NATURE: HUMANS & PLANTS

Watching my garden grow throughout the year, I'm reminded of just how vital our relationship to plants is—and how alike we are. It's quite a convenient arrangement. Plants need food, water, air, warmth, space, and sunlight, just like we do. They breathe in what we breathe out, and we breathe in what they breathe out. Plants are programmed to a twenty-four-hour cycle (circadian rhythm) like we are. Plants are food for us, and we can create nutritious compost for them.

And then there's our natural attraction to the sun—our bodies and skin crave sunlight for vitamin D production! Plants also naturally bend and turn to face the sun, a phenomenon called *phototropism*.

watermelons and pumpkins; in the case of strawberries, seeds are situated on the outside of the fruit.

TIME TO PLANT

Our sense of commitment to our gardens increases dramatically once we've planted the seeds—it sets a long and beautiful process in motion.

Before you plant, always to be sure to review your planting calendar, garden map, and the specific information you've gathered about the plants you plan to grow. Double-check whether your plants prefer to be direct seeded, or started indoors ahead of time and later transplanted outside. And always start a few more plants than you think you'll need. No matter how you choose to get your plants growing, sunlight, temperature, moisture, and soil should remain at the center of your attention.

Direct Seeding

Direct seeding is a particularly joyful part of the process (do I say that about every part of gardening?), especially if you're getting your hands into soil that you, Little Gardener, and nature have built together. Experienced gardeners can sometimes tell if the soil is warm enough to plant just by touching it. If you follow the dates in your planting calendar (based on number of weeks from your frost dates), your soil should

RECOMMENDED READING FOR BIG GARDENER

Interested in learning more about growing flowers? Eileen Powell's *From Seed to Bloom: How to Grow over 500 Annuals, Perennials, and Herbs* is an extensive and detailed guide that will show you the way!

be about the right temperature to direct seed. Soil thermometers are an easy (and fun) way to double-check and build your sensory skills.

Prior to direct seeding, watch the weather to see if heavy rains or severe fluctuations in temperature are expected in the next few days. If they are, consider delaying your planting time. If the weather has been very dry, water the soil the night before or the morning of, but at least an hour or two before planting so the water has a chance to soak in, preventing mucky soil.

Right before planting, loosen the soil up one more time. Work compost into the top few inches and then rake the bed so it's level. If you are planting in rows, use sticks or wooden stakes connected by string to mark your rows; space the rows evenly across your bed according to how much space your plants need. With the string as a guide, create furrows to the depth required by what you're planting.

Almost all vegetable seeds are planted less than an inch deep; a few prefer deeper, but it varies from plant to plant. Luckily, seed packets and some seed catalogs conveniently indicate planting depths. Generally (although not always), the larger the seed, the deeper it likes to be planted. Instructions may direct you to plant certain seeds a little deeper if you are experiencing weather that is colder than normal for your area.

PLANTING CHECKLIST

- ☐ Seeds or seedlings
- ☐ Planting instructions (usually found on the seed packet)
- ☐ Journal and pencil
- ☐ UV-resistant marker
- ☐ Twine or string
- ☐ Scissors
- ☐ Wooden stakes
- ☐ Popsicle sticks
- ☐ Ruler or tape measure
- ☐ Small watering can (with precise pour spout)
- ☐ Straw for mulch
- ☐ Trowel
- ☐ Rake

Seeding with Little Gardener

Hands are the best tools for planting seeds. The Littlest Gardeners, for whom fine motor skills are still developing, have an easier time handling larger seeds, such as peas, beans, pumpkins, and corn, while older Little Gardeners can manage small to medium-size seeds, such as lettuce, turnips, arugula, peppers, and eggplant. Carrots have very tiny seeds and can be difficult to handle at any age level—plant them only when you have your wits about you!

There are a few tricks I use to guide Little Gardeners in placing seeds the correct distance apart and to help us both keep track of how much of the row has been planted. After you've marked your row with stakes and string, use a ruler or tape measure to determine seed spacing, and then place a popsicle stick where each seed should be planted. As you plant the seeds, remove the sticks and continue down the row.

JUST FOR LITTLE GARDENER

A PUMPKIN STORY

When my brother, sister, and I were little, my dad would carve our names into pumpkins when they were small and their skin was still soft. The pumpkins would heal, leaving scars that spelled our names. We watched our names get bigger as the pumpkins grew larger, and when Halloween came, we each had a pumpkin with our name on it!

For seeds spaced farther apart, you can also use a small watering can with a precise pour spout to make a wet spot where each seed should be planted. Place one seed on each wet spot and have Little Gardener push them in to the appropriate depth.

Tuck in your seeds by covering them up and gently pressing down on the soil with a flat hand. (Does Little Gardener like to be tucked in?) Sprinkle mulch (straw is best) ever so lightly over the newly seeded area to protect the soil from drying out too fast.

Using a UV-resistant marker, label a popsicle stick to indicate what has been planted and the date that you planted it. Gently water your freshly planted seeds every day until they sprout.

Have Little Gardeners record in their journal what they've planted, in which bed it was planted, when they've watered it, and when it sprouts.

Starting Seedlings Indoors

When I have the time and space, I like starting my seeds indoors. "Pleasant" doesn't begin to describe how nice it is to have seedlings sprouting in the house when there is still snow on the ground outside. Buying seeds from a catalog lets you choose from a much larger selection of plant varieties than the seedlings that will be available at your local nurseries. Little Gardener may also find it easier to seed into containers or a tray with clearly identified cells than out on the open ground of the garden.

Be sure to use clean containers that have drainage holes. These can be plastic seeding trays, individual plastic pots, or biodegradable ones made from natural fiber. (There is also a biodegradable type called CowPots that are made from…guess what? Composted cow manure!) You can also make your own growing containers by punching holes in the bottoms of saved yogurt cups.

Place a tray underneath your containers to catch excess water. Label the tray and then plant seeds according to their instructions. Water them lightly every day. And watch for germination! Seeing your first sprouts come up is an exciting time.

Starting seeds indoors has always been worth it, but it can be a little messy, and you may need to make a small investment to get your system set up the first year. Seedlings do best when they have direct light and lots of it: ten hours or more a day. Unless you have sunny springs and a window with bright and consistent exposure, it can be difficult to grow strong seedlings, and I would recommend purchasing grow lights (or using a fluorescent light you already have).

Hang the lights a few inches above your seedlings, moving the plants lower, or lights higher, as the seedlings grow, being sure they never touch the lights. If you plan to start your own peppers, eggplants, flowers, or tomatoes, which require an early start and warm soil to germinate, a heat mat placed under your growing trays will significantly improve your—and their—growing experience. Try using a grow light without a heat mat first, as the heat from the light may be sufficient, depending on the ambient temperature.

Potting Mix
Vegetable and flower seeds germinate best in a special type of soil called *potting mix* or *seed-starting mix*. Choose a type

HELPFUL HINT
USING GROW LIGHTS

If you decide to use grow lights, you might choose to place several small blocks or boards under your plant trays and remove them as your plants grow taller. This may be easier than adjusting the height of your grow lights.

that is certified organic if that feels like a match for your values and intentions. The potting mixes I've purchased from local or regional purveyors have consistently outperformed those I've bought from large garden-supply centers. Many gardeners and aspiring homesteaders swear by crafting their own seed starting mix, but I've yet to find a home-grown recipe that does a better job for me than the regional organic suppliers I've been using. I encourage you to experiment on your own!

Seed-starting mix doesn't need to be nutrient-rich because, remember, seeds have their own built-in food tank that feeds them until they begin photosynthesizing. Rather, it serves as a medium for the plant to anchor into, promotes root development, and regulates water retention and air flow in a way that nurtures the seed.

As a newly germinated sprout becomes a seedling and continues to grow, it will use up its stored energy and start to need richer soil. A week or so after forming its first true leaves, plants generally benefit from a nutrient boost of liquid fertilizer or being repotted into a more nutrient-rich medium (a mix of potting mix and compost will suffice).

Hardening Off

Seedlings started in the comforts of ideal sunlight, water, and temperature need a slow and easy introduction to the real world that awaits them outside. Plants not given this time to adjust before being transplanted will likely experience a shock akin to a sleeping gardener being brought outside in his bed on a cold winter day and having his covers abruptly removed. Give your plants a few days outside in a sunny, semiprotected spot before transplanting them into their final garden home. While it's important that seedlings acclimate to greater temperature fluctuations and mild to moderate wind, if extreme weather or

DAMPING OFF

A common culprit for the death of small seedlings is a fungal disease called damping off, which causes the stem to decay and the seedling to fall over. Seeding into clean containers, not overwatering, and encouraging airflow (a fan in the corner of the room will do) can all help to prevent this common issue.

temperatures threaten, bring plants back inside temporarily.

Purchasing Seedlings

If you prefer to purchase seedlings, I suggest you visit a local farm nursery since staff will likely have assisted in growing the seedlings offered for sale. They may be able to tell you what growing practices were used to grow them and may even know how they will taste when mature!

Be sure to select healthy plants with thick, hearty stems and no discoloration or wilting. While it may feel counterintuitive, don't choose young plants in small pots that are already flowering or fruiting too early in the season; it may be a sign that the plants have been stressed from lack of care and are rushing to reproduce.

Transplanting with Little Gardener

When you are ready to transplant into the garden, consult your planting plan—your calendar and your map (see page 107) —to confirm where to plant. As with direct seeding, prepare your garden bed by moistening the soil in advance, and by loosening the soil and incorporating compost right before you plant. Transplanting on a mild, overcast day will reduce transplant shock.

Create your row guide, measure out plant spacing, and place popsicle sticks where Little Gardener should dig. Holes should be close to twice the size of the containers the seedlings have grown in. To remove a plant from its container, gently squeeze the sides of the container while slowly tipping it to one side so that the plant comes out into your hand. Place the plant in the hole, fill the remaining space with soil (and a little compost too, if you have some handy), and press firmly to tuck the plant in. Making a slight depression in the soil will allow water to collect near the base of the plant

HELPFUL HINT
MINIMIZING TRANSPLANT SHOCK

I've noticed little to no transplant shock when I water my transplants with a solution of Neptune's Harvest Fish Fertilizer immediately after planting. This will give your plants a boost as they adjust to their new environment. Wear clothes you don't mind getting yucky—fish fertilizer is delicious for plants but stinky for humans!

and slowly sink toward the roots. Always water the soil a plant is growing in rather than the plant itself.

Certain plants are more tolerant of being transplanted than others. Don't be too alarmed if your plants look unhappy for a couple of days after transplanting. Water them every day until they bounce back.

FROM SEED TO SEED

Most plants start as seeds and—toward the end of their life cycle—produce seeds of their own. Watching your plant's journey from seed to seed is both memorable and moving. Saving seeds to plant the following year is even more so.

As your garden progresses from seeds to mature plants, you may decide to save seeds from some of the strongest plants. As discussed earlier, some plants' seeds form inside the fruit part of the plant. (Can you remember which fruit is the exception to this "rule"?) The seeds can be removed, cleaned, dried, and stored. To collect seeds from other plants, you must let them "go to seed." For example, instead of harvesting turnips or a head of lettuce or broccoli when they are ready to eat, allow them to keep growing. They will eventually form flowers, and produce seeds that you can dry and save. And not only will *you* get some seeds, but birds will be able to enjoy some too!

It's important to note that some seeds will develop "true" to the parent plant you collected them from, and others won't. I say, experiment! Save some seeds just to see what happens and record your findings in your journal. If you have your heart set on saving seeds that grow true to the parent, avoid hybrid seed varieties. Instead, choose open-pollinated and heirloom varieties, and research how far apart to separate plots to prevent cross-pollination.

ACTIVITIES

GROWING YOUR OWN SECRET SPOT: SUNFLOWER HOUSES

(Adapted from *Roots, Shoots, Buckets & Boots* and *Sunflower Houses*, both by Sharon Lovejoy)

Sunflower houses are enchanted, jungle-like garden sanctuaries, the perfect places for Little Gardeners to play and hide in. Sunflowers of various heights and colors create a shelter and serve as a trellis for morning glories to climb. Plant your sunflower house a week or two after your average last frost. Soak your morning glory seeds in water the night before.

To start your sunflower house, you will need:

☐ A few packets of sunflower seeds that will grow to different heights (suggested varieties: 'Jade', 'Chocolate', 'Lemon Queen', 'Strawberry Blonde', 'Autumn Beauty', and 'Mammoth')

☐ A few packets of morning glory seeds (the variety 'Heavenly Blue' offers a stunning contrast to the warm yellows, oranges, and reds of the sunflowers)

☐ Compost (nice, but not necessary)

☐ Popsicle sticks

To complete your sunflower house, you will need:

☐ Twine
☐ Scissors
☐ Ladder or a step stool

1. Mark out a large rectangle, about 6 × 9 feet, on open, loose soil that gets ample sun, with one of the short sides of your rectangle facing south (north if you are in the Southern Hemisphere).

2. If you have access to compost, sprinkle a little along the perimeter and work it into the soil with your hands or a hoe.

3. Leaving a small, unplanted section for an entrance on the south side (north side if you're in the Southern Hemisphere), plant sunflower seeds 6–8 inches apart and 1–2 inches deep.

4. Interplant morning glory seeds about ½ inch deep and 6–8 inches apart.

5. *Note:* Simplify the above planting steps for very Little Gardeners by setting out seeds at the appropriate spacing, marking each spot with a popsicle stick so the seeds are easy for Little Gardener to spot and push in.

6. Water them daily until everything has sprouted, then cover the area inside the rectangle with mulch.

7. When the morning glories almost reach the top of the sunflowers, it's time to build a roof!

8. Big Gardener can climb a ladder to reach the tops of the sunflowers and tie the twine under a sunflower head. Run the twine back and forth across the top of your sunflower "room," carefully tying twine around the uppermost part of the stalks. The morning glories will expand to fill in your roof, and you'll have created a flower-filled secret garden space.

OBSERVE & DRAW THROUGH THE GROWING SEASON

Regardless of how much artistic talent you believe you have, I encourage you and Little Gardener to give this activity a try. Drawing, or even simply attempting to, tends to slow down the mind enough to help you more clearly perceive what you are looking at.

You will need:

- ☐ Your gardening journals
- ☐ Pencils, crayons, markers, or any other favorite drawing tools
- ☐ Four popsicle sticks (two for Big Gardener, two for Little Gardener)
- ☐ UV-resistant marker

1. As your first sprouts come up, each choose a plant that you would like to observe over the course of the growing season.

2. Place a labeled popsicle stick next to it so you remember it's the one you've chosen to observe.

3. At the same time, choose a small seedling in wild nature to observe. Label it with a popsicle stick too.

4. Return to each plant spot over the course of the growing season—about once a week if you can or whenever new growth inspires you—to observe and draw them.

5. At the end of the season, compare the two series of drawings: What similarities and differences do you see? What other ways can you use art to connect to the lives of plants in the garden and in the wild?

JOURNAL PROMPTS

- Which came first, plants or seeds?
- What is growing in your garden that you yourself did not plant? How is that happening?
- Why is our relationship with plants so important?

CHAPTER REVIEW

- Seeds are pure magic—they remain dormant until conditions are just right. Water them *every day* until they wake up and sprout!

- Before you direct seed (or transplant), prepare your soil, and review your planting calendar, garden map, and the specific information you've gathered about the plants you plan to grow.

- Label all your plantings (have fun and get creative!) and have Little Gardener record what they've planted in their journals.

IN THE NEXT CHAPTER...

Now that you've planted the seeds from which your garden will grow and flourish, it will need your loving attention throughout the growing season. Don't worry, nature will do some of the caretaking work for you! As you and Little Gardener learn how to steward your garden to be healthy, thriving, and abundant, you will feel even more a part of the natural systems that sustain you—one of the great joys of gardening.

CHAPTER EIGHT

CARETAKING

Steward what sustains you

If the gardener serves nature, nature will serve the garden. Or, better said by Japanese farmer and philosopher Masanobu Fukouka, "Simply serve nature, and all is well." We are meant to cocreate with nature. The more your garden design and planning mimics the mechanics of natural systems, the less work will fall to you, the gardener.

Caretaking a garden tunes us into the natural rhythms and cycles at work in our own backyards and beyond. A garden "problem" is the result of nature's resources and cycles being out of balance. The essence of problem-solving is getting nature back on track in a way that benefits as many garden stakeholders as possible.

CARETAKING—THE BASICS

The most important stakeholder in your garden is your soil. The late Toby Hemenway, an avid permaculture practitioner and author, writes in *Gaia's Garden* that "feeding the soil engages us in a partnership that benefits all." The more alive and healthy your soil is, the healthier your garden will be. The message here is not just to try to keep the plants healthy, but to keep the *soil* healthy—because that will keep *more* than just the plants healthy. Proactive soil caretaking includes: minimizing erosion,

GOOD CARETAKERS ARE GOOD OBSERVERS

You are an important part of your garden. By observing your garden carefully and often, you will learn how to take good care of it.

Use this guide to help you know what to pay attention to and how to help your garden get what it needs:

☐ Check your soil. Stick your finger into the soil to make sure it's moist. Moist soil means healthy plants.

☐ Pay attention to the weather. Cover plants to protect them from freezing temps or strong winds. During very dry or hot weather, plan to give your garden more water.

☐ Watch for garden pests. If you notice holes in the leaves of your plants, you might cover them to keep the pests out.

☐ Keep an eye out for sick plants. When a plant is sick, its leaves may get spotted or change color. When you water, water the soil instead of the leaves (some plants get sick if their leaves are wet a lot!).

☐ The most important thing to take care of in your garden is the soil. If you take good care of the soil, it will take good care of your plants.

maintaining a balanced soil rich in organic matter and soil life, and managing moisture. (See page 124 for more on taking care of soil.)

I ♥ Mulching

Of any garden caretaking activity, mulching, in my opinion, has the highest energy return on investment. Mulch is any material used to cover soil. Gardeners use a variety of materials for mulch. Leaves, straw, grass clippings, thick layers of wet newspaper, cardboard, or wood chips are all excellent candidates. Gardeners may also use what is known as *living mulch*. A living mulch is a ground cover of low-growing plants that grow beneath and around a main crop.

Mulch protects the soil from erosion, suppresses weed growth, and minimizes moisture loss due to evaporation. It also breaks down over time, adding nutrients to the soil. In my gardens, mulch consistently wins the award for "Greatest Multitasker," and, as a bonus, Little Gardeners usually enjoy "tucking in the soil" by spreading mulch.

Reduce Soil Erosion

Minimizing the loss of soil to erosion will ensure that the rich soil you've worked so hard to build doesn't needlessly disappear. Plant roots keep soil in place, so the more soil you can cover with plants, the better. Windbreaks can reduce the effects of strong winds that carry away soil as well. If you're expecting heavy rains and you have bare soil, consider putting hoops and row cover over your garden beds until you have time to plant or mulch; this will mitigate the impact of the rain on the loose soil.

COMFREY: A GARDEN WORKHORSE

Comfrey is an herbaceous perennial whose admirable qualities are numerous. It has an array of medicinal properties, the attractive flowers invite pollinators and other beneficial insects to the garden, it can serve as forage for livestock, and it grows prolifically. It is even aggressive enough to outcompete grass!

A gardener who plants a comfrey patch will have access to her own locally grown, nutrient-rich mulch. Known as a nutrient (or dynamic) accumulator, comfrey's extensive root system harvests nutrients from deep in the soil and stores them in its leaves. To make use of comfrey's nutrient-gathering superpowers, harvest the leaves and use them as mulch or green manure. You can also make a liquid fertilizer from fermented leaves. By cultivating this multipurpose plant, a gardener can let nature do a whole lot of soil enrichment work for them.

Note: I advise working with Russian comfrey, as True comfrey spreads easily by seed and may colonize areas beyond what some gardeners may be pleased with.

Watering

When watering your garden, the rule is: just enough, not too much. Moist soil encourages vibrant soil life. Where I live, an inch of rain per week keeps the soil and most garden vegetables happy. You can set up a rain gauge in your garden to measure how much nature has watered your garden.

Water in the morning or the evening to minimize evaporation in the heat of the day, especially if you live in a dry area or have limited access to water. Remember, you are watering the soil so that the soil can take care of the plant, and some plants prefer not to get their leaves wet (it's an invitation to certain plant diseases). Soil rich in organic matter that is well mulched will hold moisture even longer! Using soaker hoses can save water, time, and concentrate water right where it's needed.

Feeding the Soil That Feeds Your Plants

Maintaining soil fertility is an ongoing act of giving back to the soil. Regularly incorporating compost, replenishing mulch, and watering with worm tea—a nutritious solution made from worm casting (a.k.a. worm poop!)—will all enrich soil. You can also add green manure to your soil by turning plant matter, like grass clippings, comfrey leaves, or certain weeds, into the soil. You can leave them right on the surface too. Over a few weeks, they will degrade and release nutrients back into the soil. (Avoid using diseased plant matter, plants that are aggressive spreaders, or those that are about to go to seed.)

Cover cropping is another way to build soil fertility. While primarily used on farms and large gardens, the practice can be adapted to smaller spaces. Cover cropping is the intentional planting of an entire area with a specific crop that will be used as a green manure.

These crops, which are season specific, mitigate erosion and help retain soil moisture (and may attract pollinators too). When you turn the plant matter into the soil, it becomes infused with organic matter that feeds soil microbes.

Note: Any time you incorporate a significant amount of fresh plant matter into the soil, wait two to three weeks before direct seeding into it, as active decomposition can inhibit seed germination.

GARDEN MANAGEMENT BY THE SEASONS

Spring Rev your engines. Clarify goals. Make a plan. Order seeds. Take care of seedlings. Check fences and bed borders for winter damage and make repairs. "Open up the garden" by removing any overwintered debris. Build trellises. Plant and mulch. Maintain soil fertility. Protect plants from late frosts with row cover.

Summer All systems go. Plant, mulch, prune, trellis climbing plants, fertilize, weed, water. Plant some more! Maintain soil fertility. Mulch more. Mulch even more! Turn the compost pile regularly. Harvest!

Fall The cool-down cycle (and beginning of the next season). Harvest some more! Protect sensitive plantings from early frosts. Collect seeds and store them properly. Clean trays and planting pots. Add layers to your lasagna garden to decompose over the winter. Don't forget to plant your garlic! "Close up the garden" and protect your soil by heavily mulching.

Winter Hibernation mode. Winter is a gift of rest to a gardener, but to earn it you must spend your fall preparing the garden for hibernation. Take quiet time to review caretaking records. Make notes on what worked and what didn't. Inventory seeds. Dream about the year ahead. Put your feet up while you peruse seed catalogs.

IF & WHEN THE GARDEN FALLS OUT OF BALANCE

Problem-solving—or garden-rebalancing—is a teacher unrivalled in its ability to turn us into ecologically literate "systems thinkers."

If plants have what they need, they'll do a decent job of taking care of themselves. When you notice unhealthy plants, recall what plants need in order to grow. Is this plant receiving the amount of sun, airflow, water, warmth, space, and food it needs? Which if any of these are out of balance? How can you rebalance the system to better support the success of that plant? Sick plants may not be getting what they need to defend themselves. Providing them with it is a good deal easier than dealing with pests and disease.

Pests & Diseases

I am not an expert on plant diseases or garden pests, but I do know that the more vigorous your plants are, the better prepared they will be to handle either of these challenges. Choosing or growing strong seedlings, planting polycultures, rotating crops, watering the soil instead of the plants, and carefully removing diseased plants (and not adding them to your compost pile!) all help reduce the chance of disease.

What I do know is that everything in nature is eating everything else. To deal with pests, you can plant companion plants, including herbs and flowers, as pest deterrents. Invite ladybugs, spiders, praying mantises, and snakes into your garden for

LET IT BE

What may be an autumn eyesore of dead stalks and fallen-over plant matter to some gardeners is a paradise for birds, decomposers, and other creatures. At the end of the growing season, remove any diseased plant matter, but allow anything else to compost in place. Let Earth take it back in her own time.

backup. (See page 215 for companion planting suggestions.)

There are numerous books devoted to pests and disease and how to deal with them. Below you'll find a very quick list of some of the most common and egregious "offenders," along with the plants most often affected by them. Use this list as a jumping-off point for seeking additional information. Many agricultural extension offices have gardener hotlines where master gardeners are available to answer questions about growing, pests, diseases, and a plethora of other gardening topics.

(See page 215 for companion planting suggestions.)

HELPFUL HINT
ROW COVER

For every farm and garden I've worked in, row cover has been a dear friend and trusted ally. Also known as "floating" row cover, this lightweight fabric can be used to protect plants from frost and pests as well as provide slight shade. If a frost threatens and you're without row cover, cardboard boxes or cut-open milk jugs work great to cover individual plants overnight!

Veggies and Common Diseases that Love Them:

Beet: **leaf spot**

Beans: **anthracnose, wilt**

Cucumber: **anthracnose, downy mildew, mosaic virus**

Eggplant: **wilt**

Lettuce: **downy mildew**

Melon: **mosaic virus, powdery mildew, wilt**

Onion: **downy mildew**

Peas: **blight, powdery mildew, wilt**

Pepper: **anthracnose, sunscald***

Potato: **blight, mosaic virus, scab, wilt**

Spinach: **downy mildew, wilt**

Squash: **mosaic virus, wilt**

Tomato: **blight, mosaic virus, sunscald,* wilt**

Watermelon: **anthracnose, mosaic virus, wilt**

*Sunscald is not a disease but its effects on tomatoes and peppers can look like one.

Veggies and Common Pests that Love Them:

Arugula: **flea beetles**

Broccoli: **cabbage worms, flea beetles**

Cabbage: **aphids,* cabbage worms, flea beetles**

Carrot: **carrot rust fly**

Corn: **corn borer, corn earworm**

Cucumber: **cucumber beetle**

Eggplant: **Colorado potato beetle,** flea beetles, tomato hornworm**

Kale: **flea beetles**

Lettuce: **cutworm, slugs*****

Melon: **cucumber beetle**

Onion: **maggot, onion thrips**

Peas: **aphids***

Pepper: **tomato hornworm**

Potato: **aphids,* Colorado potato beetle,** flea beetles**

Raspberries: **Japanese beetle**

Root vegetables: **rodents**

Spinach: **leaf miners**

Squash: **squash bugs, vine borers**

Strawberry: **rodents, slugs*****

Tomato: **Colorado potato beetle,** flea beetles, tomato hornworm**

Turnips: **flea beetles**

Watermelon: **aphids,* cucumber beetle**

* encourage ladybugs
** encourage toads
*** like to come out when it's dark or cloudy

WEEDS: FRIENDS, FOOD, FOES

A weed is any plant growing where you would prefer it wasn't. The best way to handle weeds is to prevent them from even starting. If you've done a good job mulching and interplanting, weeding should be manageable. The upside of having weeds (yes, there is an upside!) is that many of the most common ones are edible,

RECOMMENDED READING FOR BIG GARDENER

THE WILD WISDOM OF WEEDS

Interested in getting more out of your garden weeds? Katrina Blair's book *The Wild Wisdom of Weeds* includes unique and delicious recipes that use common weeds as featured ingredients.

have medicinal properties, and can be used as a green manure (as long as they are not aggressive rooters or about to release their seeds).

Any weeds that aren't of use or that you don't want to proliferate should be pulled up before they go to seed and spread. In my gardens, weeds fall into three categories: friends, foes, and food. Below are some common weeds that might pay you a visit.

Friends & Food

Chickweed (*Stellaria media*) Edible, living mulch

Lamb's quarters (*Chenopodium album*) Edible, green manure

Thistle (*Cirsium* spp.) Edible, flowers are friends to bees and butterflies

Dandelion (*Taraxacum officinale*) Edible, important food source for bees

Pigweed (*Amaranthus retroflexus*) Edible, green manure

Plantain (*Plantago major*) Edible, medicinal

Purslane (*Portulaca oleracea*) Edible, green manure

Quickweed (*Galinsoga ciliata*) Fast-growing edible, green manure

Stinging nettle (*Urtica dioica*) Edible. Handle with gloves! Stinging hairs lose their sting when cooked.

Caution: Do not eat any plant you do not know unless it is positively identified by an expert. Know which parts of the plant are edible, how and when to harvest them, and how to properly prepare them.

Foes

Bindweed (*Convolvulus arvensis*)
As the name implies, bindweed wraps its vines around other plants as it climbs, and it has a strong root system. While I haven't tried it myself, I've heard that you can cut pieces of the tender vines, before they dry and become too brittle, to use as ties (like pieces of twine) for tomatoes.

Quackgrass (*Agropyron repens*) a perennial,
and **Crabgrass** (*Digitaria sanguinalis*) an annual
I've yet to discover a reason to have an affinity for these grasses in or near my gardens. I can appreciate their ambition to grow, their ability to mitigate erosion, and how they serve as habitat for soil life…just not in the garden.

MANAGING TO-DOS FROM WEEK TO WEEK

Once a week during the growing season, my Learning Garden intern and I would walk through the garden taking notes on the progress of plantings, choosing projects Little Gardeners could help us with that week, and making a ready-to-harvest list. We'd review any tasks from the week prior that we didn't get to and make notes of things that would likely need doing the week after, and even some bigger projects to save for somewhere down the line. As the season progressed, we'd also check in with our seasonal to-do list.

Taking the time to make observations on a regular basis is an essential part of effective caretaking. I loved having a good excuse to be out in the garden, knowing I wasn't there to do anything but observe and take notes. Our weekly garden walks kept us in tune with what was happening in the garden and made it easier to spot places where garden systems were out of balance.

Keeping an eye on the weather will help you stay on top of things— as will taking note of unusual temperatures, when particular pests appear, and how your plants are progressing. It's also important to keep track of how you take care of your garden each week. Employing a particular gardening method (or importing a new kind of soil or compost) one year may have ripple effects through growing seasons ahead, and, unless everything is written down, you'll have a hard time making connections between your methods and your results.

DO THE LEAST HARM

Celebrated farmer and author Eliot Coleman eloquently remarks, "The systems of the natural world are elegant and logical. The idea of striving to create life-giving foods while simultaneously dousing them with deadly poisons is inelegant and illogical."

When faced with the inevitable temptation to use a chemical product to "solve" a problem, like spraying herbicides to manage grass (which is only trying to make a good life for itself), consider the ramifications. Anything that hurts your soil hurts your garden. Killing the grass with poison could also kill soil life. Insects that might otherwise benefit your garden could suffer. Make choices that increase the resilience of your garden, not undermine it.

An engaged gardener is a creative caretaker and avid solution-seeker. When you come up against a challenge, look for solutions that create additional solutions and not additional problems. What solution can you and nature come up with that does the least harm? By getting creative in partnering with plants' intrinsic strengths, the gardener's workload lessens. Be mindful of all the work plants and insects do just by being themselves. Nature always finds a way, and so can you.

Instead of using chemicals to manage grass creeping in at the garden's edge, build time for "grass patrol" into your weekly routine, or plant something with an aggressive growth habit that can outcompete the grass—like comfrey, mint, bee balm, chamomile, or oregano. There are also businesses that will bring goats to your yard to eat down your grass and weeds. These are solutions where everyone benefits—except for the grass.

REFRAMING WORK AS JOYFUL DOING

American culture appears to have a complex relationship with the word *work*. In a zine produced by Modern Times Theater, "The Rural Person's Verbal Reclamation Front" seeks to correct "the basic assumption that (a) chore equals drudgery." Rather, they say, a "chore equals drudgery only when the task is imposed by a third party," and notes that "without that imposition, drudgery remains drudgery, but chore becomes… a blow for freedom."

Work only really means "doing." To engage children in joyful garden "doings," it's critical to create and promote verbal contexts that disassociate garden maintenance from the unfortunate negative implications of work or chores. Instead, we must model that the purpose of physical "doings"—in the

NATURE'S WAY OF MAINTAINING

In ecologist Allan Savory's studies of African grasslands where grazers had been absent, he notes, "The stems and leaves produced last growing season by these grass plants are now dead and will block sunlight from reaching the plants' ground-level growth points. Unless this old material is removed before the coming growing season these plants will produce very few new leaves." His point is that for the grass to effectively reproduce, grazing animals need to be present to eat the grass, and return nutrients to the soil in the form of manure. One could say that grazers help maintain the system, but really it's just grazers being grazers, living things doing what they do.

garden and elsewhere—is to create greater well-being for humans and the environment, illustrating that work is really "caretaking."

Through play, cultivating curiosity, and offering the promise of a snack, you can get the Littlest Gardeners to appreciate the garden and connect with it, and once this happens, they will want to take care of it. Children may not want to "work," but they often enjoy being helpful—the negative connotations of work haven't even entered into the equation.

Parents are often surprised when I report what great "work" their child did in the garden that day. After children have had positive experiences caretaking, it's important for them to hear that they've done great "work." In this moment, a small step is taken to redefine work as being helpful or taking great care of something, and drudgery's parasitic grip begins to loosen.

The language we use is significant. Experiment with avoiding using the words *work* and *chores*, at least in the beginning. Instead, try saying, "Let's go check on the 'preschool' peppers and see if they need anything," or "I bet the melons are thirsty—let's bring them a drink." Observe how Little Gardener responds.

Expressing "garden exasperation" to Little Gardener will not help this cause. Even if the weeds have taken over and it's a busy week, do your best to model garden anticipation, excitement, and curiosity, and remember that mistakes are okay. There is no such thing as perfect when it comes to gardening.

HELPFUL HINTS
CARETAKING WITH EASE

Gardening can be hard work (even with nature's help)! Here are some tips to make caretaking easier on you and Little Gardener.

- ☐ To make crossing over wide beds easier, add stepping stones where needed (especially for Little Gardeners with a short stride).

- ☐ Always have row cover on hand to protect your plants from pests or frost.

- ☐ Longer tool handles mean less bending. Keep your garden tools easily accessible, and brush them off before you put them away.

- ☐ Let the water drain out of your garden hoses before moving them.

- ☐ Make or purchase a kneeling pad. Low gardening seats are handy too (some have wheels so you can scoot along without needing to stand up!).

- ☐ Put tools and supplies away last, or you'll be running to the shed for something you've already put away.

- ☐ Have a hose repair kit on hand!

- ☐ Weeding after rain makes for easier work.

- ☐ Shake excess soil from your weeds before hauling them off. Your soil is precious, don't let it leave your garden on the roots of weeds!

ACTIVITIES

GARDEN OLYMPICS

Garden Olympics is a great activity for a weekend afternoon. It can amp up the energy, especially between siblings, around any number of garden tasks. Here are some ideas for healthy contests:

- Who can collect the most garden pests? (Are there any neighborhood chickens you could feed them to?)

- Who can be the first to fill their bucket with weeds?

- Who can find the biggest peas that are ready to harvest?

You can create a weekly score sheet and add up points at the end of the growing season! In the end, though, the garden is the real winner.

YOUR WEEKLY GARDEN CHECK IN

Observation, recording, and reflection, while they might sound a little boring at first, are the most valuable and rewarding things Big Gardener and Little Gardener can do as stewards of the garden. Here's a way to make caretaking together even easier:

1. Add a weekly garden walk to your planning calendar. Bring copies of your garden map (one for each of you!). While observing the garden, note on the map where it needs help. Let your notes be your caretaking guide for the week.

2. Discuss how you will both work together to take care of the garden that week. What roles will you each play? What roles will nature play?

3. In your journals, reflect on how nature has contributed to the success of your garden since your last walk. (Maybe your compost is ready to use, and the worms and microbes could use some recognition. Maybe you can thank your pollinators because your melon flowers have fruits starting to form.)

4. Once you become experts at the weekly plan, create an annual caretaking plan on your garden calendar. What reminders can you set up for yourself to help remember how your garden needs you?

JOURNAL PROMPTS

- What work did you do in the fall, winter, and spring to make summer caretaking less challenging?
- How does nature take care of you? (Do you or your family take any medicines or vitamins that are derived from something in nature?)
- What challenges did you experience in maintaining your garden this year?
- How might you change your garden design, annual plan, or growing strategies to make caretaking easier?

CHAPTER REVIEW

- Take good care of your soil! The more alive and healthy your soil is, the healthier your garden will be.

- An engaged gardener is an avid solution-seeker. When faced with a challenge, look for solutions that benefit you, the garden, and the earth.

- Reframing work as "joyful doing" will encourage Little Gardener to be an active caretaker.

IN THE NEXT CHAPTER...

Throughout the growing season, take time to simply visit and observe the garden. Set an intention to do *no work* of any kind during these times. You'll develop an even deeper relationship with what you are cocreating with nature. Besides, you can't make every moment in the garden about caretaking. You need to save room. For dinner. Finally, let's eat!

CHAPTER NINE

HARVESTING

Experience nature as food

Isaac stood up from the garden beds with a smile as he added peppers to the harvest basket. He glanced up at me and then looked out across the Learning Garden. "This is great. We're outside. It's a beautiful day. And we're picking vegetables."

I smiled too and looked up. "It *is* pretty great, isn't it."

On days like this, surrounded by the garden's abundance, recognizing that we belong to nature is as easy as breathing. Isaac, in third grade, had perfectly summed up what gardening is all about—at least for me. On those beautiful days, or even brutally cold rainy ones, when you pick vegetables and eat them, there is a mindfulness to it—a slowing down of body and mind that gifts you a distinct variety of awe. In these raw moments, we feel more alive.

I cannot count the number of times I've seen a child in total shock as they pull a carrot out of the garden soil. They look at the carrot with wide, wild eyes as if to say, "How is this even possible?" It is possible because you and nature are designed to work together and take care of each other.

FIRST HARVEST

Every year, gardeners wait patiently for their first harvest; it's the culmination of all the visualizing, discovering, navigating, designing, planning, planting, growing, and caretaking. First harvests are special no matter how long you've been gardening, but if this is your very first year gardening, make a big deal out of it. Celebrate all the work you, Little Gardener, and nature have done together. Go to the garden to taste the bounty, and don't forget to record the date in your journal so you have more information for next year.

How do you know when your vegetables are ready?

Even if you've never grown tomatoes before, I trust you to do a decent job of knowing when they're ready. You already know what a ripe tomato looks like, and your body will probably *want* to eat them.

Think of how vegetables look in the grocery store. While they probably don't look as fresh as what you've grown, they can give you an idea of the size, shape, and colors to expect. If you've been carefully and regularly observing the progress of your garden, you'll start to notice when your vegetables are almost ripe. Until your garden instincts fully develop, you can also check your planning calendar for a general idea of when each of your plantings may be ready.

RECOMMENDED READING FOR LITTLE GARDENER

Plants Feed Me **by Lizzy Rockwell is a fun and easy-to-read book that introduces Little Gardeners to how plants grow and the different plant parts we eat.**

HELPING LITTLE GARDENER
HARVEST CAREFULLY

It's easy to imagine Little Gardener accidently pulling up a whole lettuce plant when the intention was to harvest only one leaf. Here are a few kid-friendly (and plant-friendly) harvest techniques:

Steady Hand, Picking Hand This stand-by technique can be used for just about every harvest maneuver involving the fruits of a plant (including but not limited to peas, beans, cucumbers, melons, peppers, and tomatoes). The nondominant hand is the steady hand that holds a plant or its branch in place to keep it from being pulled up or snapped unintentionally. The dominant hand is the picking hand, which pulls (and maybe gently twists) the fruit away from the steady branch.

Caterpillar Fingers This easy method will help Little Gardener find the right place to sever a stem of kale, chard, spinach, leaf lettuce, and the like. First, find the leaf you want to pick. From the tip of the leaf, walk down the stem with your fingers to just above where it meets the ground or the main "trunk" of the plant. For thick stems, twist and pull. For tender stems, use the "lobster pinchers" method.

BEFORE GARDENS

Long before we began growing fruits and vegetables from cultivated gardens and farms, humans acquired their food by hunting animals and gathering plants from wild nature. Many of our modern-day cultivated crops are descendants of wild ancestors. While it's not the way most people get the majority of their food today, people do still hunt animals and forage for plants and mushrooms.

Lobster Pinchers To properly break tender stems, like those of spinach, arugula, and lettuce, use your Caterpillar Fingers to walk down the leaf. Sever the stem just above the ground by pinching the tips of your forefinger and thumb together and gently pulling the leaf.

Fingertip Pluck Where only minimal effort is required to remove a small fruit, as with cherry tomatoes or raspberries, use only your thumb and forefinger to delicately pluck it from the plant.

Root Harvesting Loosen the soil in advance with a digging fork. Grasp what you're harvesting (for example, carrots or turnips) as low as possible. Position your arms and shoulders directly above the vegetable and pull straight up with steady force.

To Wash or Not to Wash

When Little Gardeners and I would walk through the garden, exploring and tasting the vegetables, fruits, herbs, and flowers that were ready to be picked, they would often ask, a bit alarmed, "Shouldn't we wash what we pick before we eat it?"

Rinsing produce before you eat it is a sound practice that I'm not here to talk you out of. When you grow your own organic vegetables, however, there are no pesticides to wash off, and no lingering contaminants or germs from being handled by people during cross-country travel. If my vegetables have soil or bugs on them, I give them a rinse—not because soil or insects are dirty, but because having grit in my teeth is no fun.

GETTING KIDS (& ADULTS) TO TRY NEW FOODS

Upon greeting visitors to the farm and Learning Garden, I'd always start off by asking, "Who likes to eat?" Hands and sounds of enthusiasm would shoot up over the tall-backed bus seats. "Great, because today is all about food!"

Picky eaters were not difficult to identify. Among the excited majority, there were always a few pairs of eyes that filled with dread when I said, "Today is all about trying new things. Do you think you can be brave eaters?" Most obliged, but some, including adult chaperones, clearly felt uncomfortable and anxious about eating vegetables and were vocal about it.

My most disheartening moments in the Learning Garden were often the result of adult comments like, "I don't know why anyone would eat beets, they're disgusting," or "I don't eat vegetables because I don't like them." Perhaps they didn't have access to fresh produce where they lived or never had the opportunity to learn cooking techniques that might make vegetables more appealing. But given that the focus of the program was tasting and cooking with garden vegetables, I was often surprised by the adults in the group—assuming, regardless of their veggie affinity, that they had my back in encouraging their children to try fresh food.

My carefully crafted response to the occasional anti-vegetable outburst is, "Well, we all have different food preferences, and that's great, but living bodies need living food to be healthy." I'd also introduce our funny Learning Garden tasting motto, "Don't yuck my yum," a saying I'd picked up years earlier from a fellow educator. We would tell students, "We all have different taste buds, and that's okay, but it's not okay to make someone feel bad about what their taste buds tell them."

Big Gardener, this is a friendly reminder not to let your likes and dislikes needlessly color Little Gardener's palate. Children are constantly gathering information about everything they are hearing, seeing, and experiencing. And, as we all know, they do a magnificent job modeling adult behavior, attitudes, values, and comments.

HELPFUL HINT
BE PREPARED FOR SNACK TIME

Keep harvest baskets, a harvest knife, and a small cutting board easily accessible for impromptu snack attacks and garden taste tests.

Enthusiastically share your opinions about different foods with Little Gardener, but do so without "teaching" Little Gardener what they should or should not like. If you don't like a particular vegetable, eat it anyway, even if only once, to model that you can still try things you don't like—both to show Little Gardener that doing so isn't the end of the world and to check to see if your own taste buds have changed.

The Peanut Butter Cup Analogy

Each summer, through the height of the growing season, we would lead hundreds of kids, parents, and teachers, through our tomato jungle, a hundred-foot-long greenhouse filled with cherry tomato plants six to eight feet tall. The long corridors of vining plants were often three or more times taller than our littlest visitors.

"Do you know what these are?"

"Cherry tomatoes!"

"Yes! Cherry tomatoes. These are the most delicious cherry tomatoes I have ever had, and we're going to taste some."

I was a picky eater growing up (sorry, Mom!) and can empathize with the children on the bus who panicked as they

CHANGING TASTE BUDS

Do you know that your taste buds change as you grow up? An easy way to see if you like something you've never tried before, or to see if your taste buds have changed, is to do a taste test.

You can even taste test different varieties of the same vegetable, because each variety has different flavors. You might like the flavor of one variety but not the flavor of another. But you'll never know until you try it! When you do a taste test, make a note in your journal about what you like or don't like about the taste or texture.

Is there anything you love to eat now that you used to say "yuck" to? What do you think you might like when you're older that you don't like right now? By trying new things all the time, you won't miss out on a new favorite!

felt the pressure of being pushed outside their food comfort zones.

"Is anyone feeling a little nervous about trying this? It's okay if you are! You can be honest." Some hands would apprehensively go up.

A student would inevitably say that they had already tried cherry tomatoes and that they didn't like them, to which I'd respond, "Well, you've never tried our cherry tomatoes before, the ones from this farm. Plus, taste buds change, so I want everyone to be brave and give it a try."

Before we'd start, I'd ask them to raise their hands if they liked peanut butter cups. Predictably, almost all hands would go up.

"Now, what if I told you I'd never had a peanut butter cup in my life — that I'm scared to try it and I already know I don't like it. How would you get me to try it?"

"We would tell you it's delicious!"

"What if I still didn't want to try it? What if I didn't believe you?"

"You just have to try it. You will like it!" they'd respond.

"So, say I agree to try it and nibble the tiniest bit off the edge, and I decide right away that I don't like it. Am I really getting the whole idea of what a peanut butter cup is if I just nibble the edge?"

"No! You have to bite into it!" they would stress.

Holding up the cherry tomato, I'd say, "While this is not a peanut butter cup, cherry tomatoes have an outside and an inside too. If I just nibble at the skin like this, am I really tasting the tomato?"

"No!"

"That's right—the juiciest, tastiest part is inside! Give it a chance, just like tasting more than the edge of the peanut butter cup. Be brave and bite into it. Ready to try?"

Given this analogy, and with the caveat that they could spit it out after taking a real bite and a couple of chews, eight or nine out of every ten Little Gardeners would try the cherry tomatoes. Without it, we could usually get six or seven to take the leap of faith. And almost everyone who tried one liked it. An eight-year-old Little Gardener named Blessing remarked after tasting cherry tomatoes, "They are so sweet, I would eat them for breakfast, lunch, dinner, *and* dessert."

GARDEN TO TABLE—PREPARING & COOKING THE FRUITS OF YOUR LABOR

When children participate in the growing and preparation of fresh food, they are more likely to eat it. Through planting seeds, taking care of the garden, and then harvesting and cooking fresh produce themselves, Little Gardeners understand that healthy soil grows healthy food that can be crafted into delicious, healthy meals.

In the Learning Garden, we encouraged our Little Gardeners to "walk like farmers and think like chefs," and imagine what they might create from the vegetables, fruits, herbs, and flowers surrounding them. With the guidance of our chefs, students would create a farm-fresh lunch in our outdoor kitchen just steps from the garden, using ingredients they'd harvested themselves. And, very often, they were surprised to discover that they actually *did* like some vegetables.

OUT OF THE MOUTHS OF BABES

"I DON'T LIKE EATING VEGETABLES, BUT I LIKE EATING THIS."
— Chase, age eight, while visiting Wyomanock Center for Sustainable Living and eating zucchini and onion sauté with parmesan cheese

"THIS FOOD MAKES ME WANT TO GET UP AND DANCE."
— Sha-He, age seven, after tasting salad with shredded carrots and honey lime cilantro dressing during cooking class

"MY MOM IS NEVER GOING TO BELIEVE THAT I LIKE ASPARAGUS."
— Summer-camp student at The Sylvia Center

Have you ever noticed that food seems to taste better when you eat it outside? Why do you think that is? I'm convinced it's because something special happens in our bodies when we are eating nature out in nature.

Cooking with the Seasons

Cooking with garden produce helps Little Gardener chefs understand that fruits, vegetables, and herbs are available seasonally, or at certain times of the year. Spring brings asparagus, rhubarb, sugar snap peas for snacking, and spinach for salads. In the summer, salads may include ten different types of greens garnished with edible flowers of borage, calendula, and Johnny-jump-ups, and dressings made from perennial and annual herbs. Fall root vegetables, including carrots, beets, and turnips, can be roasted or made into soups, stews, and chilis. Cabbage, also harvested in the fall, can be saved as a winter storage crop and made into crunchy slaw. Butternut squash can be stored well into winter and incorporated into cakes and soups.

The Farm Chef Challenge

Each summer at The Sylvia Center's Young Chefs Farm Camp, we would host a "Farm Chef Challenge." Teams of students would be presented with five surprise ingredients that they would need to use in an original recipe. With the garden and a pantry of spices and other staples at their disposal, they created a dish that was judged on flavor, teamwork, creativity, presentation, and technique/execution.

Fun activities like these help Little Gardener chefs gain confidence in their ability to experiment with flavor and prepare food by learning safe cutting techniques and age-appropriate cooking methods. I encourage you to create your own version of this activity at home! Kitchens, like gardens, are dynamic environments where sensory-based, hands-on, experiential learning happens naturally.

Parts-of-a-Plant Salad

When we eat vegetables from our garden, we eat different parts of different plants. Depending on the type of plant, we may eat the roots, stems, leaves, flowers, fruits, or seeds.

When we eat spinach, what part of the plant are we eating? The leaves. When we eat a radish, what part of the plant are we eating? The root! When we eat a pepper, what part of the plant are we eating? The fruit. When we eat peas, what part of the plant are we eating? The seeds.

At The Sylvia Center, we would make a salad where each ingredient comes from a different plant part. You can too! A "Parts-of-a-Plant Salad" might include a leaf (such as lettuce), fruit (such as tomato), flower (such as nasturtium), bud (such as broccoli), root (such as carrot), stem (such as celery), and seeds (such as corn kernels). How many different parts of a plant can you find in your garden to include in your salad?

Add your favorite salad dressing or experiment with a brand new recipe.

RECOMMENDED READING FOR GARDENING FAMILIES

In *Sylvia's Table: Fresh, Seasonal Recipes from Our Farm to Your Family*, written by Liz Neumark with Carole Lalli (and inspired by The Sylvia Center), you'll find many delicious, garden-fresh, family-friendly recipes. Some Little Gardener favorites are Chunky Purple Potato and Leek Soup, Kale Crisps, Baked Stuffed Zucchini Boats, Oven-Baked Apples, and the Sylvia Center Frittata!

ACTIVE GRAZING: HARVESTING & EATING AT THE SAME TIME

Produce begins breaking down right after it's been picked—as the time between harvest and consumption increases, the nutritional value of fruits and vegetables decreases. Smart post-harvest care practices and refrigeration slow this process, but the fact remains that the sooner you eat something, the juicier, more flavorful, and more nutritious it will be.

It would then follow that the best arugula I can eat from the garden would be arugula that I pluck from a growing plant with my own mouth. I can't think of a more efficient way to decrease the amount of time between harvesting and eating than to harvest by eating!

One summer morning on the mesa at Tomten Farm, there was a gentle consistent mountain breeze, snow-covered peaks in the distance, sun shining bright, and a bluebird sky above. I glanced around the garden and lowered myself to the earth. Mindfully, I brought my face down into the arugula patch and took it all in. Close to the ground, I could see greater detail, smell a more robust earth scent, and observe the distinct way the light hit and almost shined through the arugula leaves. Using my mouth like lobster pinchers, I carefully took one arugula leaf from the plant and chewed it slowly, convinced it was the most tender, delicious, and nutritious piece of arugula I'd ever eaten. It was great. It was a beautiful day. And I was picking vegetables.

ACTIVITIES

TASTE-TEST PICNIC

Cucumbers are my favorite vegetable (fruit, actually!) to taste test with Little Gardeners. While different varieties of cucumber have green, yellow, white, or orange skin, the differences in flavor and texture are so subtle between varieties that it challenges Little Gardeners to pay very close attention to the tasting experience.

You will need:

- ☐ Blanket
- ☐ Cutting board
- ☐ Knife
- ☐ Napkins
- ☐ Your journals and writing implements
- ☐ A few varieties of cucumber (or any vegetable you wish) that you will pick from your garden (or supplement from a farm stand or grocery store).

1. You're having a picnic! Bring a blanket, cutting board, a knife, napkins (and cucumbers you may have purchased) to the garden.

2. If you've grown multiple varieties of cucumbers (or any other fruit or vegetable), pick one of each kind.

3. Take a seat somewhere comfy in the garden, slice up your cucumbers, and taste each variety one at a time.

4. Compare the different varieties, describing and rating them for flavor, texture, and appearance. Give each kind an overall thumbs-up, thumbs-down, or sideways thumbs (for "just okay") rating. Share which varieties you like best and why.

5. Based on the preferences you've both discovered, make notes in your journals that will help you decide which varieties to grow more or less of next year.

Extra Credit: The next time you and Little Gardener are at the grocery store, count how many different varieties of cucumbers (or any vegetable) there are to choose from. Compare it to the number of varieties offered in seed catalogs. What do you notice?

UNUSUAL EATING

I'd like to challenge you and Little Gardener to explore eating nature in a different way.

Start off by actively grazing in your garden! Find something in your garden that you are able to harvest with your mouth instead of your hands—such as a leafy green, a cherry tomato, or an edible flower. This is a fun way to get *really* close with your garden and experience the way many other animals on Earth eat!

You can also seek out a local expert to take you and Little Gardener foraging for berries, nuts, greens, and mushrooms. Eating from wild nature is an experience you will never forget.

JOURNAL PROMPTS

- What is the most delicious thing you've harvested from the garden this year? The most beautiful? The most unusual?
- What grew the best in the garden this year, and why do you think this was so?
- Beyond growing food and providing nourishment, how does nature contribute to our survival?

CHAPTER REVIEW

- Teach Little Gardener kid-friendly (and plant-friendly) harvesting techniques, such as lobster pinchers, caterpillar fingers, and more.

- Encourage adventurous eating, and remember the helpful phrase, "Don't yuck my yum!"

- When children "walk like farmers and think like chefs," their excitement around growing and eating fresh food—including vegetables!—multiplies.

- Harvest season is the perfect time to help Little Gardener gain confidence in the kitchen, where they can learn safe cutting techniques and age-appropriate cooking methods.

IN THE NEXT CHAPTER...

It doesn't get much better than eating what you, your family, and nature have grown together. Humans are meant to cocreate with nature, and when the result of that partnership is a full belly, the experience is that much more satisfying. Gardens serve as vibrant learning spaces through which Little Gardeners can come to understand the natural systems that exist beyond the garden's boundaries—and how those systems sustain us and all other life on Earth. As a Big Gardener, you are in a unique position to become nature's teaching assistant so that Little Gardener can become nature's keeper.

TEACHING & LEARNING IN YOUR GARDEN

CHAPTER TEN

GROWING A LITTLE GARDENER

Teach yourself to guide the way

When guiding children through the Learning Garden, I often began our journey by exploring herbs. Even the most apprehensive students could usually work up the courage to pinch off a few leaves of parsley or a sprig of thyme, crush it up between their fingers, and smell it.

I had been working on developing and experimenting with a short inquiry-based narrative to introduce a particular herb. One summer day, I decided to try it with twelve elementary-school students. We paused on our walk through the garden and circled up around one of the herb spirals.

I instructed the students to gently pluck one leaf from a particular herb (using their lobster-pinchers), crush it up with their fingers, and hold it just under their noses. "Today," I told them, "is about walking like a farmer and thinking like a chef." Then I asked them, "When we use herbs and spices in cooking, do we use a lot or a little?"

"A little," some students answered.

"Why only a little?" I inquired.

"It might be too spicy or strong."

I explained that when we taste herbs by themselves, those with sensitive taste buds may find them strong and off-putting. Instead of tasting, smelling the crushed herb can actually give us a better idea of what flavor it will impart on the ingredients it's mixed with. Then I asked, "When you smell this herb, do you think it would be a good flavor match with your favorite sandwich?"

One student responded, "I think it would not go good with my peanut butter, banana, and honey sandwich." Another was eager to report that she thought it would go well on her grilled cheese and tomato sandwich.

"Okay, what about tomato sauce? Do you think this herb would go well with tomato sauce?" Affirmatives. "Do you think it would go well on pizza?" Almost all yeses.

"How many of you have ever been to a pizza place?" All hands go up. "And have you ever noticed those shakers on the table with extra stuff you can sprinkle on your pizza? There's usually a few of them."

"Yeah, sometimes I sprinkle the red spicy one on mine!" announced one student excitedly, while others nodded and acknowledged having seen or used the shakers.

"Ah, yes, there's usually hot pepper flakes. And what about the other shaker on the table, the one that looks like dried leaves crumbled up small?" Silence. "I'll give you a hint, it's the herb you're holding in your hand right now!" Silence.

Things were not progressing as I had expected—the discussion was losing momentum, and I was about to lose their attention. My educator brain quickly recalculated my approach. In an "emergency" such as this, and particularly with younger students, I often revert to the simplistic and not particularly creative tactic of offering the hint "It starts with an *O*," hoping everything will click.

One hand immediately and exuberantly shot up, the small human jumping up and down, "Oooo, oooo, I know, I know!" Relieved, I called on him.

"OCTOPUS!!!" he reported with serious pride.

I don't recall exactly how I responded in the moment, but I hope it was no more than a silent sigh and a gentle smile.

We then practiced saying "oregano" a few times while smelling it again and imagining how it would taste on pizza. Despite our circuitous path, the end result was that a previously unknown and nondescript plant was now connected to pizza—something so pervasive and well-known that they might just remember it.

Experimenting like this helps teachers (and Big Gardeners) develop an internal gauge for age appropriateness. We got to the conclusion eventually—in a more roundabout way than I'd hoped for, but that's what the adventure of teaching is all about. Crafting strategies to guide Little Gardeners toward figuring out answers on their own is an endless challenge, and an incredibly fulfilling one.

CULTIVATING CONNECTION

Creating joyful, authentic, conscious connections between people and the natural systems that sustain them is my life's purpose. Simply spending time outdoors nurtures these connections, but in gardens specifically designed to engage children through play, exploration, cocreating with nature, and eating what they've helped grow, they occur readily.

After spending just one morning in the Learning Garden, sparks are flying between Little Gardeners and the garden itself, and there is a palpable energy shift in the group. They have room to breathe and the freedom to move at nature's pace; there's a little more room for being mindful of one's place in the world. Little Gardeners begin to feel how their own lives are intertwined with the life of the garden. It's an enlivening wake-up call to the fact that they are part of nature—because they see that they can grow, pick, and eat it.

There are some things we just know—things we feel in our bones. We don't need a study to tell us that broccoli is better for us than gummy bears—we feel it. And we don't need a study to inform us that spending time outside is healthy for our minds and our bodies. We can feel that, too. We instinctively know that spending all day inside is not what we were built for. Instinctively, we feel and know that our own well-being is inextricably tied to the well-being of the earth.

But sometimes we need reminders. Garden-based education delivers these. Crafting gardens as alternative classrooms gives people of all ages, abilities, and learning styles an opportunity to refresh their memory of their connection to the Earth. Because Earth is nature, and nature is food.

MY APPROACH TO GARDEN-BASED EDUCATION

One of my favorite pieces of wisdom for teaching, learning and life, comes from Kyle Cease, a comedian, author, and motivational speaker who writes, "The moment that we do the thing is when we learn how to do the thing."

I do not have a formal education in education as a field. And while there may be crucial nuts and bolts missing from my educational pedagogy and my knowledge of child development, learning to teach by striving to teach has laid a more than adequate foundation. Nature has always been the lead teacher, and I've only ever had to be the assistant and a guide. The dialogue that happens between nature and children is one that happens without much prompting from me—as a Big Gardener, I simply help guide the conversation.

Too often, the structure of formal lessons, the strict rules of curriculum, testing standards, and time constraints can suppress the innate curiosity that helps children learn on their own. Unstructured and self-directed play and exploration are marginalized in favor of relative stillness and the confines of classroom walls. While I've certainly found some "sit-down" lessons to be effective, both in my time as a student and as an educator, learning about the way the world operates by participating in the way the world operates seems infinitely more sensible than any other approach.

I can't comment from direct experience on the efficacy of formal lessons from a classroom teacher's perspective, but from my experience as a student in both traditional and nontraditional settings, I can tell you that learning in a classroom was no match for learning holistically—with my whole body in real time.

If we are to form meaningful connections to the things of this world and learn deeply from them, we must fully surround and engage ourselves with them. When children are immersed in real life, they learn about real life. They learn colors by way of flower gardens, painting, drawing, and mixing hues. They learn history through stories told and written by people who lived through it, perhaps more easily than through textbooks written by people who did not. They learn basic math through cooking or carpentry (or gardening!). They learn the nature of soil by creating soil. Everything has a basis in the natural world. Find it. Leave the walls behind.

TEACHING PHILOSOPHIES

Experiential education, place-based education, inquiry-based learning, and "unschooling" are the teaching and learning philosophies I've found to be most valuable in cultivating Little Gardeners as nature's keepers.

Each methodology places an emphasis on learning through diversified experiences that support the full range of learning styles. Of course, these approaches are not mutually exclusive— they can easily be combined and used with other teaching methods. More like members of a collaborative ecosystem or a family of educational models, these philosophies focus on students' roles in their own learning.

Experiential education is founded on the theory that learning happens best when the setting and, more importantly, the experience of that setting is the actual subject matter—the direct experience of the subject is how we learn about it. This methodology emphasizes the relationship between hands-on learning and real-world outcomes.

Place-based education seeks to cultivate a holistic and interdisciplinary sense of place that students can use as a template for understanding other places and communities. Using their unique set of local resources, educators facilitate the building of relationships between students and their communities, both human and ecological. Students who know

LEARNING STYLES

Copious studies have been conducted and many theories have been developed on how we learn. Each theory categorizes and names learning styles differently, but of the classifications I've come across, these from Michigan State University are the most clear and comprehensive to me.

Visual: learns best through seeing

Aural: learns best through hearing and music

Verbal: learns best through words (speaking, reading, writing)

Physical: learns best through senses and by using the body

Logical: learns best through reasoning

Social: learns best by working in groups

Solitary: learns best by working alone

Learning happens differently for each of us, and the way in which we learn changes over time as our brains develop. People learn by engaging a combination of these strategies, but typically one or two will stand out as dominant. Each learning style "lives" in a different part of the brain, and the more parts of the brain that are engaged in learning, the better we will retain the information from our experiences.

What are your and Little Gardener's primary learning styles? Which of the activities and parts of the creation process in this book did you connect with and learn from the most? What learning opportunities can you craft to meet both of your needs?

their places well have a strong foundation when it comes to understanding other places and people.

Inquiry-based learning focuses on awakening children's natural sense of wonder and encouraging them to craft their own line of questioning. Anatole France's nineteenth-century quote sums up beautifully the intention of an inquiry-based learning strategy: "The whole art of teaching is only the art of awakening the natural curiosity of young minds for the purpose of satisfying it afterwards." By presenting questions and real-world scenarios before "facts," the teacher paves the way for a student-led path to discovery.

"Unschooling," popular with homeschooling networks and families, honors a child's interests and curiosities by allowing those curiosities to define what knowledge the child will pursue. Children have an innate desire to learn; unschooling lets them do it at their own pace and by following their own interests.

In addition to these recognized approaches, educators also have their own gut instincts at their disposal. Paying attention to a child's responses to varied learning environments, stimuli, and scenarios; sensing where they are and meeting them there; and modeling what being an active learner looks like will all enrich your own unique approach to guiding Little Gardener in their learning.

Gardens offer interdisciplinary educational opportunities and cater to multiple learning styles. Whenever you feel excited to teach Little Gardener something about the world, ask yourself, how can the garden be the teacher? How can I facilitate Little Gardener's learning by being the teacher's assistant?

(A GUIDE TO) BECOMING LITTLE GARDENER'S GUIDE IN THE GARDEN

The garden itself will be Little Gardener's primary teacher. As Big Gardener, you are tasked with helping that relationship flourish.

As you select an activity or develop your own, I invite you to choose one or more of the following "educator mindsets" to embody; experiment with these approaches as you teach and learn together in the garden:

Be patient and flexible.

"Be the guide on the side, not the sage on the stage"—student-driven learning is far more effective than being talked at.

Let Little Gardener's interests be your guide. Let go of what you expect to happen. You never know what will ignite something in a student; may your communications be authentic and lively.

Make your enthusiasm visible. A teacher's genuine excitement is contagious. Be sure to express it.

Wear time loosely. Let the garden be a place for both structured and unstructured time. (But mostly unstructured time!)

Be positive and uplifting, and let your sense of humor shine through.

Ask one question at a time, and be specific.

Express gratitude for the garden and what you receive from it.

Take advantage of activities centered on play (for the Littlest Gardeners), exploration (for medium-size Little Gardeners), and action (for bigger Little Gardeners).

Demonstrate joyful problem-solving—simply modeling what being an active learner looks like is an undervalued form of teaching.

Cultivate curiosity, then get out of the way.

Welcome mistakes. Mistakes are okay. Be sure Little Gardener knows this without a doubt.

EMBRACING UNCERTAINTY

It's a beautiful spring day. You and Little Gardener walk into the garden intending to plant lettuce and pea seeds. You've got your garden map, you've got your ruler. The soil feels just right. You start to think that you should probably build a pea trellis before planting the seeds, so you run back to the shed for twine and wooden stakes.

In the time it takes you to travel those ten steps, the wind picks up your open packet of lettuce seeds and scatters them across the garden as it sees fit. Or, perhaps, while you were gone, your Little Gardener scattered the seeds as she saw fit. Let it be. Let the seeds grow where they will. Laugh about it. Watch to see where the seeds sprout and count how many days it takes.

One year, you will have amazing carrots. The next year, heavy rains will wash the seeds away the day after you plant them. The following year, you will have amazing carrots. You plant the turnips in the "wrong" spot. Little Gardener harvests all of them too early. Let it all go. Let it all be.

A bird's nest nestled in the herb spiral steals the excitement from the first hot pepper ready to be picked for the salsa you've been dreaming of since spring. In that moment, redirect yourself to focusing on harnessing Little Gardener's spontaneous and authentic interest in the bird's nest rather than trying to force his attention on the pepper. Save the pepper for later. You will both enjoy your time more.

Children and nature are unpredictable. Taken together, they are an unstoppable force; no two things are more adept at setting a stage for complete uncertainty. But we can be grateful for that uncertainty, because for any frustration it may cause adults, it inspires undying curiosity in children. The unknown holds dynamic spaces for learning.

It has taken me a long time to accept that I can only claim so much responsibility for the success or failure of my gardens and what children learn from them. Ecological systems and a child's natural curiosity tend to operate independently of our efforts.

We never do know how each season's dance with nature will turn out. In the age of having endless information available so quickly and easily, gardening is an excellent lesson for Little Gardener, and perhaps for Big Gardener too, in embracing the unknown—a living spark resides there. And living closer to nature brings that spark more intimately into our day-to-day lives.

Kyle Cease also reminds us to "choose to fall in love with not knowing what is going to happen." I'll add "when gardening with kids" to the end of that.

ACTIVITIES

SPEAKING OF LEARNING...

It's time for you and Little Gardener to reflect on, and share with one another, how you each learn. Before starting the conversation, consider the following questions:

- What qualities have your most valued and significant teachers and mentors shared? Who were they? What did you learn most from them?

- What have been some of your favorite and most memorable experiences with learning?

- What can a teacher do to turn something seemingly boring into something that's exciting for you? How do you learn best?

- How can a teacher help you recall and integrate what you've learned?

Share some of your thoughts and stories from the above list with Little Gardener (if you like, prepare a snack from the garden to enjoy while talking together).

Invite Little Gardener to tell you stories about their favorite teachers, with the reminder that teachers aren't just in classrooms—they can pick anyone they've learned from.

What memories do they have of learning something exciting? You might have something in mind, but let them lead the conversation as much as possible.

How can you take what you've gleaned from your conversation into the garden, your "unclassroom"?

SHARING WITH YOUR COMMUNITY

Through the process of dreaming up a garden and making it real, you've learned so much. How can you share with others what you have learned about gardening and the process of creating your garden? Here are some ideas:

- Ask Little Gardener's schoolteacher if you and Little Gardener can share your gardening experience (and a snack from your garden) with the class.
- Invite friends and family over for a garden party. Let Little Gardener give a tour. Serve snacks made with ingredients grown in your garden. Show garden pictures that you've drawn.
- Grow extra plants in pots and give them as gifts. Label them and include simple care instructions.
- Start a local gardening club in your neighborhood or help a neighbor start a garden.
- Talk to teachers or the principal at Little Gardener's school about having a school garden (even if it's just a small container garden).

JOURNAL PROMPTS

- What is your favorite way to learn in the garden? By watching first? By doing?
- What is your favorite way to teach in the garden? Show and tell? Working side by side?
- What have you learned about yourself as a garden teacher and a learner?
- How has the garden helped grow Little Gardener?
- How have you and Little Gardener grown closer by teaching and learning in the garden together?

CHAPTER REVIEW

- Children and nature are unpredictable—embrace the uncertainty that is part of cocreating with nature and Little Gardener!

- When it comes to gardening, teaching philosophies that focus on letting Little Gardener lead the way do the best work of cultivating nature's keepers.

- Understanding Little Gardener's (and your own) learning styles will help you use your garden as a teaching tool.

- The garden will be Little Gardener's primary teacher. As Big Gardener, your vital role is to help that relationship flourish.

LOOKING AHEAD...

Every year, my garden and the Little Gardeners I work with teach me so many new things. My garden teaches me how to build healthier and healthier soil. It shows me how I can tune into the seasons even more deeply. The Little Gardeners teach me how to be a better garden teacher and learner. They teach me how to be a better person. As the growing seasons come and go, you and your Little Gardener will learn more about gardening, the natural world, and each other too. Relish every moment of it.

CONCLUSION:
THE CULTIVATED, THE WILD, AND YOU

Often, what we learn to appreciate, know, and value develops as a result of larger cultural and community expectations. I've seen far more natural spaces become box stores and parking lots than I've seen box stores and parking lots become natural spaces. I recognize that this is a little oversimplified, but I think often of the impression that this commonly held value might make on our children, our Little Gardeners.

Author Richard Louv articulates it well in his book *Last Child in the Woods*:

> Parents, educators, other adults, institutions—the culture itself—may say one thing to children about nature's gifts, but so many of our actions and messages—especially the ones we cannot hear ourselves deliver—are different. And children hear very well.

Our failure to prioritize ecological systems shows young people just how "unimportant" those systems are; and those choices will perpetuate the myth of our independence from nature. This is how walls are built. Educators can limit how tall and strong they become by modeling something different.

We are of wind and water, of sun and soil. Has there not been just one moment in your life when the wind or sun on your face felt like home, the sound of a river balanced you out, or touching bare earth made you feel at one with it? A time when the taste of a sun-warmed strawberry made the world slow down?

I am grateful to have had the opportunity to connect with nature, and feel one with it, countless times. I am more grateful to have seen children feel it too. The profound joy and fullness of life experienced in moments like these is challenging to replicate indoors.

Gardens awaken our instinct to cocreate with nature, and the way we feel when we recognize it is raw and alive. Our relationship with nature is sacred, and food is the most visceral part of that relationship. Food helps restore memories of a connection that we seem to have forgotten.

A sense of belonging is essential to human happiness. We tend to assume this applies only within our human communities, but it also means we must recognize and honor our ties to our ecological communities. Not regularly experiencing these connections to nature—through food, water and wind, sun and soil—is a heartbreaking loss. A loss of day-to-day peace, well-being, and belonging; a loss for the culture of our communities; and a loss for all creatures who are directly and indirectly affected by our lack of connection.

I could not know my whole self without the conscious connections that living closer to nature brings. I imagine there are many Little Gardeners who would grow to feel the same way but may never have the opportunity. By cocreating your own sustenance in harmony with natural systems, you and Little Gardener will experience an Earth connection—in the words of Thoreau—"unexpected in common hours."

It is my heartfelt hope that your garden will foster a deep and lasting relationship between you and the ecological systems that keep you, and all life on this beautiful planet, alive and well. May your garden invite you in, bring you joy and wellness, and inspire you and Little Gardener to be nature's keepers.

FINAL JOURNAL PROMPTS

Bringing a garden to life is an amazing journey. As a way of marking and reflecting on your first year as gardeners, both Big Gardener and Little Gardener can read through the prompts below—separately or together—and respond in your journals to the ones you connect mostly deeply with. Then share with one another as you wish:

How have you and your garden grown?

- What has been your favorite part(s) of having a garden?

- How has designing, creating, planting, caretaking, and harvesting a garden changed you? How has it helped you?

- Describe how your relationship with your garden has changed or affected your relationship with nature as a whole.

- What are your best memories from the process of bringing your garden to life?

- Make a free associative list of what you've learned from your garden through the seasons (include both gardening facts and deeper learning).

- How have your intentions and desires for your garden changed over the course of this process?

- How has your relationship with your backyard changed over time?

- How has your knowledge of and your relationship to soil, wind, water, insects, or plants grown?

If you could go back in time...

- Would you design the layout and structures of your garden any differently?

- Would you plan the "what, when, how much, and where" any differently?

- Would you change how you constructed your beds?

Reflecting on your first season...

- Was there anything about your space that you didn't notice in your initial observation that you noticed later in the growing season? What effect did it have in your garden, if any?

- What roles did you play in the garden ecosystem over the course of the growing season? What roles did nature play?

- How are you a part of your human community much like a plant is part of its ecological community? How can you become even more connected to both communities?

RESOURCES

COMPANION PLANTING GUIDE

PLANT	"FRIENDS"	"ENEMIES"
Asparagus	basil, nasturtium, parsley, tomato	onion (*Allium*) family
Bean, bush	most vegetables, strawberry, summer savory	onion (*Allium*) family, fennel
Bean, pole	carrot, corn, radish, summer savory	beet, *Brassica* family, onion (*Allium*) family, sunflower
Beet	most members of the *Brassica* family, bush bean, lettuce, onion	pole beans
Broccoli (*Brassica*)	aromatic herbs, beet, onion, potato	pole bean, tomato, strawberry
Cabbage (and many other *Brassicas*)	aromatic herbs, bush bean, beet, celery, chard, kale, lettuce, nasturtium, onion, potato, spinach, thyme	pole bean, strawberry, tomato
Carrot	bean, chive, lettuce, onion, parsley, pea, pepper, rosemary, sage, tomato	dill, celery, parsnip
Cauliflower (*Brassica*)	celery, also see Cabbage	strawberry, tomato
Celery	bush beans, cabbage, cauliflower, leek, tomato	carrot, parsnip
Corn	bean, cucumber, melon, pea, potato, pumpkin, squash	tomato
Cucumber	bush bean, cabbage, corn, lettuce, nasturtium, pea, radish, tomato, sunflower	aromatic herbs, potato
Eggplant	bean, pepper	fennel
Kale (*Brassica*)	cabbage, aromatic herbs	tomato

Kohlrabi (*Brassica*)	aromatic herbs, beet, cucumber, lettuce, onion	pole bean, strawberry, tomato
Leek (*Allium*)	carrot, celery, other members of onion (*Allium*) family	bean, pea
Lettuce	basil, beet, cabbage, carrot, cucumber, onion (*Allium*) family, radish, strawberry	none
Melon	corn, radish, sunflower	potato
Onion (*Allium*)	beets, *Brassica* family, carrot, lettuce, parsnip, pepper, strawberry, tomato, turnip	asparagus, bean, pea
Pea	aromatic herbs, bean, carrot, celery, corn, cucumber, potato, radish, turnip	onion (*Allium*) family,
Pepper	basil, carrot, eggplant, okra, onion, parsnip, tomato	none
Potato	bean, cabbage, corn, horseradish, marigold, pea	cucumber, pumpkin, tomato, turnip, squash, sunflower
Pumpkin	corn, eggplant, radish	potato
Radish	pole bean, carrot, cucumber, lettuce, nasturtium, parsnip, pea	hyssop
Spinach	cabbage, strawberry	none
Squash	corn, nasturtium, radish	potato
Strawberry	borage, onion, sage, spinach, thyme	cabbage
Tomato	asparagus, basil, carrot, celery, cucumber, marigold, mint, nasturtium, onion, parsley, pepper	*Brassica* family, corn, fennel, potato
Turnip (*Brassica*)	pea, onion (*Allium*) family	potato
Watermelon	potato, radish	none

EDUCATIONAL ORGANIZATIONS & RESOURCES

Bioneers Hub for innovative solutions to environmental issues, and connects people with each other and the planet. bioneers.org

Center for Ecological Literacy Offers educational programming that encourages and promotes sustainable living. Many resources available for educators. ecoliteracy.org

Children & Nature Network Dedicated to making sure all children have access to nature in their everyday lives. childrenandnature.org

Cornell Garden-Based Learning Provides educational programming for all ages, as well as teaching resources and professional development opportunities for garden-based educators. gardening.cals.cornell.edu

The Edible Schoolyard Project Brings edible education (gardening, cooking, and healthy eating) into schools. Many resources for educators. edibleschoolyard.org

Farm-Based Education Network (FBEN) Supports farm-based education initiatives by offering educational programs for educators and providing a platform for networking and resource sharing. farmbasededucation.org

Kids Gardening Offers gardening guides, activities, and other resources for educators looking to connect children to nature. kidsgardening.org

Life Lab National leader in the garden-based learning movement. Offers garden educational programs, resources and professional development for educators. lifelab.org

Shelburne Farms Offers programs for students and educators focusing on sustainability. shelburnefarms.org

The Sylvia Center A nutrition and youth development organization working in high-need, high-potential communities to help young people establish healthy habits leading to happier lives. sylviacenter.org

GARDENING INFORMATION & SUPPLIES

Cooperative Extensions Search for your local extension offices and land grant universities here: https://nifa.usda.gov/land-grant-colleges-and-universities-partner-website-directory

Gardener's Supply Company Extensive garden supply offerings. gardeners.com

Lehman's Supplies for gardening and outdoor living (including Little Gardener–sized gardening tools!) lehmans.com

Mother Earth News Bimonthly magazine about all aspects of sustainable living with a focus on organic gardening. motherearthnews.com

National Gardening Association Gardeners' networking organization. Many instructional videos. garden.org

The Permaculture Podcast Weekly podcast exploring all aspects of permaculture through interviews with leaders in the field. thepermaculturepodcast.com

Rodale Institute Leading research institute for organic gardening and farming. Also offers educational programs, books, and other resources. rodaleinstitute.org

United States Department of Agriculture Producer of the USDA Plant Hardiness Zone Map. https://planthardiness.ars.usda.gov/PHZMWeb/

United States Environmental Protection Agency Producer of the fact sheet: "Reusing Potentially Contaminated Landscapes: Growing Gardens in Urban Soils." https://www.epa.gov/sites/production/files/2014-03/documents/urban _gardening_fina_fact_sheet.pdf

SEED SOURCES

These are seed companies I have ordered from (and had great results with) annually. They offer a variety of seed options including non-GMO, organic, conventional, biodynamic, hybrid, open-pollinated, and heirloom varieties. Look for seed libraries, exchanges, or companies that are local to you; they may carry seeds specially adapted for your region.

Baker Creek Heirloom Seeds Unusual varieties. rareseeds.com

FedCo Seeds Offers smaller seed packets for small-scale gardeners. fedcoseeds.com

High Mowing Seed Company All organic. highmowingseeds.com

Hudson Valley Seed Company Beautiful seed packets. hudsonvalleyseed.com

Johnny's Selected Seeds Fastest shipping. johnnyseeds.com

Maine Potato Lady Non-GMO potato, onion, and garlic seed. mainepotatolady.com

Turtle Tree Seed Company All biodynamic. turtletreeseed.org

BIBLIOGRAPHY

Barell, John. *Developing More Curious Minds*. Alexandria, VA: Association for Supervision and Curriculum Development, 2003.

Bartholomew, Mel. *Square Foot Gardening with Kids*. Minneapolis: Cool Springs Press, 2014.

Berry, Wendell. *The Gift of Good Land*. San Francisco: North Point Press, 1981.

Blair, Katrina. *The Wild Wisdom of Weeds*. White River Junction, VT: Chelsea Green Publishing Company. 2014.

Borie, Kathleen Bond, and Gwen W. Steege, eds. *Just the Facts: Dozens of Gardening Charts — Thousands of Gardening Answers*. Pownal, VT: Storey Books, 1993.

Brady, Nyle C., and Ray R. Weil. *The Nature and Properties of Soils*. 13th ed. Upper Saddle River, NJ: Prentice Hall, 2002.

Bubel, Nancy. *The New Seed-Starters Handbook*. Emmaus, PA: Rodale Press, 1988.

Cease, Kyle. *I Hope I Screw This Up*. New York: North Star Way, 2017.

Coleman, Eliot. *The New Organic Grower*. 2nd ed. White River Junction, VT: Chelsea Green Publishing Company, 1995.

Davis, Maggie Steincrohn. *Caring in Remembered Ways*. Blue Hill, ME: Heartsong Books, 1999.

Dewey, Caitlin. "A Growing Number of Young Americans are Leaving Desk Jobs to Farm." *The Washington Post*, November 23, 2017. https://www.washingtonpost.com/business/economy/a-growing-number-of-young-americans-are-leaving-desk-jobs-to-farm/2017/11/23/e3c018ae-c64e-11e7-afe9-4f60b5a6c4a0_story.html

Foster, Catharine Osgood. *The Organic Gardener*. New York: Knopf, 1972.

France, Anatole. *The Crime of Sylvestre Bonnard* (vol. 1 of *The Works of Anatole France*). Translated by Lafcadio Hearn. London: J. Lane, 1909 (1881). Accessed June 2, 2019. Project Gutenberg. http://www.gutenberg.org/files/2123/2123-h/2123-h.htm

Friedman, Rose, and Justin Lander. *"The Rural Person's Verbal Reclamation Front."* East Hardwick, VT: Modern Times Theater, 2007.

Fukuoka, Masanobu. *One Straw Revolution*. Edited by Larry Korn. Translated by Larry Korn, Chris Pearce, and Tsune Kurosawa. New York: New York Review of Books, 1978.

Grigsby, Susan. *In the Garden with Dr. Carver*. Chicago, IL: Albert Whitman & Company, 2010.

Growing Lots Urban Farm. "Growing Lots Urban Farm: About Us." Accessed December 27, 2018. https://www.growinglotsurbanfarm.com/about

Hemenway, Toby. *Gaia's Garden: A Guide to Home-Scale Permaculture*. White River Junction, VT: Chelsea Green Publishing Company, 2000.

Hobbs, Jude, Marisha Auerbach, Rick Valley, and Anna Wemple. *Permaculture Design Certification Course*. Course, Lost Valley Education Center, Dexter, OR, December 4-16, 2014.

Kaufman, Rachel. 32,000-Year-Old Plant Brought Back to Life—Oldest Yet. National Geographic. February 23, 2012. https://news.nationalgeographic.com/news/2012/02/120221-oldest-seeds-regenerated-plants-science/

Kuhn, Dwight. *More than Just a Vegetable Garden*. Englewood Cliffs, NJ: Silver Press, 1990.

Lanza, Patricia. *Lasagna Gardening*. Emmaus, PA: Rodale Press, 1998.

Libman, Kimberly. *Growing Youth Growing Food: How Vegetable Gardening Influences Young People's Food Consciousness and Eating Habits*. Applied Environmental Education & Communication 6, no. 1 (April 25, 2007):87-95. https://doi.org/10.1080/15330150701319388

Louv, Richard. *Last Child in the Woods*. Chapel Hill: Algonquin Books, 2008.

Lovejoy, Sharon. *Roots, Shoots, Buckets & Boots*. New York: Workman Publishing, 1999.

———. *Sunflower Houses*. New York: Workman Publishing, 2001.

Lowenfels, Jeff, and Wayne Lewis. *Teaming with Microbes*. Rev. ed. Portland, OR: Timber Press, 2010.

Martin, Deborah L., and Grace Gershuny, eds. *The Rodale Book of Composting*. Emmaus, PA: Rodale Press, 1992.

Mattern, Vicki ed. *Gardener to Gardener Seed-Starting Primer & Almanac*. Emmaus, PA: Rodale Inc., 2002.

McAleese, Jessica D., and Linda L. Rankin. *Garden-Based Nutrition Education Affects Fruit and Vegetable Consumption in Sixth-Grade Adolescents*. Journal of the American Dietetic Association 107, no.4 (April 2007):662-65. https://doi.org/10.1016/j.jada.2007.01.015

Michigan State University. "Learning Styles." Accessed May 25, 2019. https://www.canr.msu.edu/od/uploads/files/PD/Learning_Styles.pdf

Peterson, Lee Allen. *A Field Guide to Edible Wild Plants of Eastern and Central North America*. Boston: Houghton Mifflin Company, 1977.

Raymond, Dick. *Garden Way's Joy of Gardening*. Charlotte, VT: Garden Way Publishing, 1982.

Riotte, Louise. *Carrots Love Tomatoes*. 2nd ed. North Adams, MA: Storey Publishing, 1998.

Roach, John. "Methuselah Palm Grown From 2,000-Year-Old Seed is a Father." *National Geographic*, March 24, 2015. https://news .nationalgeographic.com/2015/03/150324-ancient-methuselah-date-palm -sprout-science/

Rodale, J. I., Robert Rodale, Jerome Olds, M. C. Goldman, Maurice Franz, and Glenn F. Johns eds. *The Organic Way to Plant Protection*. Emmaus, PA: Rodale Press, 1966.

Rodale, J. I., Robert Rodale, Jerome Olds, M. C. Goldman, Maurice Franz, and Jerry Minnich. *The Encyclopedia of Organic Gardening*. Emmaus, PA: Rodale Books, Inc., 1959.

Sanders, Robert ed. *A to Z Hints for the Vegetable Gardener*. Charlotte, VT: Garden Way Publishing, 1976.

Saunders, Allen. "Life is What Happens to Us While We Are Making Other Plans." Chappaqua, NY: Reader's Digest, January 1957.

Savory, Allan, with Jody Butterfield. *Holistic Management*. 2nd ed. Washington, D.C.: Island Press, 1999.

Shein, Christopher, and Julie Thompson. *The Vegetable Gardener's Guide to Permaculture*. Portland, OR: Timber Press, 2013.

Skelly, Sonja M., and Jayne M. Zajicek. *The Effect of an Interdisciplinary Garden Program on the Environmental Attitudes of Elementary School Students*. HortTechnology 8, no.4 (January 1, 1998):579-583. https://doi.org/10.21273/HORTTECH.8.4.579

Skelly, Sonja M., and Jennifer Campbell Bradley. *The Growing Phenomenon of School Gardens: Measuring Their Variation and Their Affect on Students' Sense of Responsibility and Attitudes Toward Science and the Environment*. Applied Environmental Education & Communication 6, no.1 (April 25, 2007):97-104.

Sobel, David. *Beyond Ecophobia*. Great Barrington, MA: The Orion Society, 1996.

———. *Mapmaking with Children*. Portsmouth, NH: Heinemann, 1998.

———. *Place-Based Education: Connecting Classrooms and Communities*. Great Barrington, MA: The Orion Society, 2005.

Stamets, Paul. *Mycellium Running*. New York: Ten Speed Press, 2005. https://doi.org/10.1080/15330150701319438

Svetlana Yashina, Stanislav Gubin, Stanislav Maksimovich, Alexandra Yashina, Edith Gakhova, David Gilichinsky. "*Regeneration of Whole Fertile Plants From 30,000-Year-Old Fruit Tissue Buried in Siberian Permafrost.*" Proceedings of the National Academy of Sciences of the United States of America 109, no. 10 (March 6, 2012) 4008-4013 https://doi.org/10.1073/pnas.1118386109

The Sylvia Center. "The Sylvia Center." Accessed April 15, 2019. www.sylviacenter.org

Thoreau, Henry David. *Walden*. Boston: Beacon Press, 2004 (1854).

Tomecek, Steve. *Dirt*. Washington, D.C.: National Geographic Society, 2002.

Tozer, Frank. *The Organic Gardener's Handbook*. 2nd ed. Santa Cruz: Green Man Publishing, 2016.

———. *The Vegetable Growers Handbook*. Santa Cruz: Green Man Publishing, 2008.

United States Census Bureau. "Measuring America: Our Changing Landscape." December 8, 2016. Accessed May 31, 2019. https://www.census.gov/library/visualizations/2016/comm/acs-rural-urban.html

Vobejda, Barbara. "Agriculture No Longer Counts." *The Washington Post*, October 9, 1993. https://www.washingtonpost.com/archive/politics/1993/10/09/agriculture-no-longer-counts/944c2f2c-98f9-4f5e-aeac-d3160cb0993a/

Yost, Bambi, and Louise Chawla. *Benefits of Gardening for Children*. Children, Youth and Environments Center for Research and Design. University of Colorado at Denver and Health and Sciences Center, August 2009. Accessed May 25, 2019. https://www.academia.edu/6169311/

ACKNOWLEDGMENTS

Much like gardening, crafting a book is a labor of love. *The Little Gardener* grew thanks to the creativity, expertise, and generosity of so many people.

Whenever I'm outside teaching, I feel grateful for Dr. Ric Campbell, Hank Colletto, and Mark Pearson, teachers who connected me with the world beyond the classroom; Dr. Charlie Hall who directed my attention toward the global environment; Dr. Rick Beal who gave me my first job in environmental education; and Reed Chambers, Julia Goren, Jen Kretser, and John Stowell for modeling what exceptional outdoor education looks like. Thanks to them, and to the many educators, farmers, interns, and Little Gardeners I've worked with over the years, I've become a better teacher and a more perceptive gardener.

Gratitude (and big hugs) to my sister, Susan Cerny, a farmer and teacher who provided insightful feedback and encouragement; Angie Hartofilis who carefully critiqued the manuscript and helped bear the burden of its "growing pains" (all while raising three Little Gardeners); Anna Hammond who entrusted me with the Learning Garden and has been a mentor ever since; Nate Landry who took such good care of me and endured my diverted attention for months; Erika Lesser, without whom my aptitude for "wordsmithing" would be far, far less; Jenn So, who reviewed my drafts and provided moral support and exceptional meals; Joan Quilty, who contributed valuable feedback on every chapter in *record* time; and The Sylvia Center staff for their enthusiastic support.

To all who shared resources, offered encouragement, or were otherwise part of the journey, thank you: Liz Baird, Susan Ball, Robyn Bosch, John H. Cerny, Hannah Fries, the Holstrom Family, Kristen Jovanelly, Karen J. Martin, Rosa McIver, Liz Neumark, Thom Pecoraro, Denise Pizzini, Taya Schulte, Bob Walker, and my extended family.

Working with the team at Princeton Architectural Press has been a pleasure and a privilege. I was glad to have Kristen Hewitt and Kevin Lippert's expert assistance, and am particularly indebted to Jennifer Lippert, whose imagination sparked the idea for the book. Heartfelt thanks to Ben English for his design talent and Ysemay Dercon for her vibrant illustrations. I would have been utterly lost without Laura Didyk's editing expertise, round-the-clock guidance, and *supreme* patience—my gratitude for her efforts cannot be measured.

The continuous support (and excited outbursts) from my parents, Carol and John, were crucial. Special thanks to my mom for being my first teacher and for reminding me that "good enough" is perfect, and to my dad, for sharing his love of gardening with me, even before he—or I—knew that I would love it too.

Published by
Princeton Architectural Press
202 Warren Street
Hudson, New York 12534
www.papress.com

Printed and bound in China
23 22 21 20 4 3 2

ISBN 978-1-61689-860-1

Editor: Laura Didyk
Designer: Benjamin English

Special thanks to:
Paula Baver, Janet Behning, Abby Bussel,
Jan Cigliano Hartman, Susan Hershberg,
Kristen Hewitt, Stephanie Holstein,
Lia Hunt, Valerie Kamen, Jennifer Lippert,
Sara McKay, Parker Menzimer,
Wes Seeley, Rob Shaeffer, Sara Stemen,
Jessica Tackett, Marisa Tesoro,
Paul Wagner, and Joseph Weston
of Princeton Architectural Press
—Kevin C. Lippert, publisher

Library of Congress Cataloging-in-
Publication Data available upon request.